Why Believe

Why Believe

by
David A. Palmer

PLACE TO GROW
PRESS
2018

Scripture quotations are from the New Revised Standard Version Bible, copyright © 1989 the Division of Christian Education of the National Council of the Churches of Christ in the United States of America. Used by permission. All rights reserved.

Copyright © 2018 by Dr. David A. Palmer

All rights reserved. This book or any portion thereof may not be reproduced or used in any manner whatsoever without the express written permission of the publisher except for the use of brief quotations in a book review or scholarly journal.

Printed in the United States of America

First Printing, 2018

ISBN 978-1-7321245-3-0

Place to Grow Press
1435 East Main Street
Kent, OH 44240

www.KentMethodist.org

Contents

INTRODUCTION VII
WHY THE ANCIENTS ALL BELIEVED 1
PROVING GOD 9
IN THE BEGINNING GOD .17
THE ARTISTRY OF GOD. .25
GOD IS GOOD 33
THE SPIRIT BEARS WITNESS WITHIN US 41
GOD'S WORD IS A LAMP. 49
WHY IS GOD HIDDEN. 57
THE LEAP OF FAITH 65
TRUE BELIEF 71
BELIEF MATTERS 77
THE WAY, THE TRUTH, AND THE LIFE 87
EPILOGUE 93
NOTES 97

Introduction

Perhaps the most famous Time magazine cover was the one from April 8, 1966, which was emblazoned with three words: Is God Dead? The magazine explored the decline of belief in contemporary culture, which had gotten to the point that several theologians launched the "death of God" movement, which was an effort to do theology without God. This was not successful.

The report of God's death was premature. Nevertheless, belief in God has been under steady pressure—assailed by atheists and skeptics, and marginalized by the culture. Is there solid reason to believe in God? How can one know? Is there any way to be sure?

Modern people are not the first to ask such questions. For centuries people have grappled with, or doubted, the reality of God; and in the process, there has emerged an extensive series of answers to the question, "Why believe?" This volume will explore those answers, and the insights they can bring to the contemporary person who wonders about God.

Abram passed through the land to the place at Shechem, to the oak of Moreh... Then the Lord appeared to Abram, and said, "To your offspring I will give this land." So he built there an altar to the Lord, who had appeared to him. From there he moved on to the hill country on the east of Bethel, and pitched his tent, with Bethel on the west and Ai on the east; and there he built an altar to the Lord and invoked the name of the Lord. (Genesis 12:7–8)

Why the Ancients All Believed

On a hilltop in Turkey called Göbekli Tepe lies one of the most important archaeological discoveries in recent years. It is an ancient temple site, consisting of circles of large standing stones, similar to Stonehenge, but thousands of years older. It is also more elaborate than Stonehenge — including intricate carvings — and it is much larger. It was built before 9000 BC, constructed on the top of a hill. This was before metal tools, before pottery, before the wheel, before developed agriculture. The people who built it were Stone Age hunter-gatherers. Hundreds of them had to work together for extended periods, using stone tools and multi-ton blocks of stone, to create this major place of worship.

Göbekli Tepe illustrates the primacy of religion in human development. The people who constructed this impressive complex were eking out their existence in a very simple lifestyle, yet they considered it to be worth enormous effort to build a grand religious center. Archaeologists used to think that people must have built cities first, and then temples followed. But Göbekli Tepe was built as people were still semi-nomadic, living in the most basic dwellings.

In fact, this pattern is not unique but can be found throughout human history — people have established permanent places of worship long before they had permanent homes. This is reflected in the Biblical story in the account of Abraham. As Abraham journeyed, living a nomadic life, he built a series of altars. The book of Genesis recounts that he built an altar at Shechem (Genesis 12:7), at Bethel (Genesis 12:8), at Hebron (Genesis 13:18), and at Mount Moriah (Genesis 22:9). The same pattern continues on a grand scale across human cultures around the world. Everywhere people have built temples and established sacred sites; and even as people began to live in cities, their religious centers were typically more prominent than anything else constructed. It all reflects the fact that human beings, as far back as one can trace, have been deeply religious, and have placed religious practice at the center of life.

Every ancient culture believed in God. There were differing conceptions of divinity, often involving multiple divine powers; but from all that archaeologists and anthropologists have been able to observe, *every* ancient culture was religious — believing in a Divine Reality beyond all things and responding in worship.

This is remarkable, considering that ancient cultures developed in widely different places and times. How can it be that cultures in the Americas, in Africa, in Europe, in Asia, and in the Pacific all came to the same fundamental religious perception — that there is a God (or gods) and that one can and should relate to God through forms of worship? As numerous researchers have observed, it is as though human beings are "hard-wired for God."

The denial of God appears quite late in the development of civilization. There are no clearly recorded incidences of atheism earlier than the sixth century BC. In the west, beginning with Xenophanes (sixth century BC), some Greek philosophers began to question traditional ideas of divinity, although often they were critiquing the Greek pantheon while still affirming a supreme Being. In the east, Buddha (sixth–fifth century BC) outlined a salvific path that left God out of the picture, but Buddha professed more of an agnosticism than an outright atheism. There is even a reference to atheism in the Bible—in Psalm 14, which begins, "The fool says in his heart, 'There is no god.'" This again is dated by most scholars to the sixth or fifth centuries BC, although others would date it to around 1000 BC (the time of King David), which would make it the oldest reference to atheism in existence! Today, some writers claim that such cases show that there was "ancient atheism."[i] Yet while it is helpful to realize that atheism is not a purely modern phenomenon, it must be recognized that the first millennium BC is not very "ancient" when speaking of the development of the human race! From Göbekli Tepe to Xenophanes is almost four times the span as the distance between Xenophanes and today; and there were many millennia of human religion prior to Göbekli Tepe. Since the dawn of time until relatively recent ages, human beings, no matter what their setting, have been fundamentally religious.

How is one to account for this? One common approach is to suggest that ancient religions were explanatory—that for ancient people in a perplexing universe, religions were an attempt to explain natural forces such as sunshine or events such as major storms by attributing them to the gods. But this theory does not at all account for the sort of faith one sees in the Bible, because the Bible does not *explain* much of anything. The Bible provides an expansive window into the faith of the ancient people of Israel, stretching back to 2000 BC and beyond, a time when human beings struggled to explain a great deal. Yet although God is affirmed in the Bible as the Creator, there is no attempt to explain natural phenomena, or the events that unfold in human lives. When Abraham is called to leave his homeland and go to the Promised Land, there is no explanation for why he has been called, or why he is supposed to go to Canaan, or why he is promised that he will have many descendants and then does not have a child for years. And when it comes finally in the Bible to the most perplexing question of all—Why do bad things happen to good people?—the answer given, in the book of Job, is that such things are beyond human comprehension. In the Bible, no one is motivated to come to faith to get explanations.

Another suggestion to try to account for the widespread human belief in God is that religion perhaps is an effort to get benefits. In this view, people looked to the gods in order to get good crops or a large family or a healing. Certainly across all religion there is a sense that God is the source of blessing, and so a natural component of religion is to seek divine assistance. But again, if one looks at Biblical faith, one finds that people do not come to belief in God because they think it is going to pay off. To the contrary, in many cases, a serious devotion to God carries a cost. Abraham gave up a comfortable life in order to follow God's call to become a wandering nomad. Moses likewise embarked on a difficult path when he answered God's call to deliver the people of Israel out of slavery; and the disciples of Jesus would enter into the costliest path of all. Serious faith does not view God as some sort of Santa Claus.

Perhaps the most common suggestion today to try to account for religion is the idea that religion arose as an effort to find an answer to death. People, it is argued, turned to religion in the hope of thereby gaining eternal life. But this theory is completely denied by the Biblical story, because for most of Old Testament history, the people of Israel did not believe in life after death. When the Old Testament speaks of "the heavens," it is talking about the sky. There is no concept of "heaven" or "hell" as a place where people might go when they die. It is only in late passages, in the years leading up to Jesus, that people begin to get a sense that perhaps God would open the way into life beyond death. Through the majority of the Old Testament story, the ancient Hebrews believed that death is simply the end of life. "All go down to the dust," says Ecclesiastes 3:20. If the Israelites tried to envision the realm of the dead at all, they envisioned it as a Pit that they called Sheol—a dark realm where the dead are nothing but a shadow. As the book of Ecclesiastes put it, "There is no activity or thought or knowledge or wisdom in Sheol, to which you are going." (Ecclesiastes 9:10) Clearly, for ancient Israelites, religion was not a way to get oneself into eternal life!

If belief in God does not explain things, and if it does not necessarily bring earthly benefits, and if it does not bring life beyond death, why did ancient Israelites believe in God? They believed in God for the same reason that they believed in the sun and the moon and the mountains and the sea — because God was a Reality that they encountered in life.

When scholars have deeply studied the origin and nature of religion, they have concluded that religion generally has this origin — in a fundamental awareness of God. Perhaps one should not even use the word "God" at this juncture, because this awareness is deeper than any of the ideas that people have about God. Rudolf Otto, in his seminal book, *Das Heilige* (*The Idea of the Holy*), used the term, "the numinous," from the Latin word, *numen*, meaning divine presence or power, to indicate what people were encountering. He noted that at the heart of every religion is this sense of the Other — not simply another being, but something very different and far greater. He called it *mysterium tremendum et fascinans* — the dreadful and yet attracting mystery. Human beings perceive this ultimate Reality that is both terrifying and at the same time beneficent. This is why the Bible regularly speaks of people responding to God with the "fear of the Lord" — fear in this case indicating a sense not of being afraid but of being in awe.

This dynamic is very evident throughout the Biblical story. From Abraham to Moses to the Biblical prophets, people come to faith because they encounter God, and that encounter is enveloped in mystery. They respond to this encounter in awe and worship. Moses takes off his shoes and shields his face when encountering the Divine in a burning bush.

Abraham and his successors build altars. Göbekli Tepe is a large-scale version of what Abraham did—building a place of worship in response to the Holy.

It is after the encounter with God that ideas about God develop—ideas about morality and eternity and the attributes of God. Theological ideas can be quite diverse, and some of them are shaped by considerable human speculation. But religion itself does not arise from speculation; it comes from a profound spiritual awareness of an Ultimate Reality—an awareness shared by human beings of every place and time.

If human beings are inherently religious, why did atheism begin to emerge in human societies around the sixth century BC? It is possible, of course, that some Stone Age individuals had doubted God much earlier, and there simply is no record of it! But there does seem to be a pattern whereby atheism grows as civilization advances. This pattern has been especially notable since the Renaissance. Is it perhaps the case that as human beings become more embedded in the trappings of civilized life, they become less conscious of spiritual reality?

Yet even as some proclaim doubt about God, religious belief has shown remarkable resilience up to the present day. The greatest example of this has been the story of faith in the Soviet Union and Communist China, where the central governments in the twentieth century undertook aggressive campaigns to completely eliminate religion. The Communist government seized all religious property, executed religious leaders, taught children to deny and ridicule religion, and severely repressed religious practice. If the "death-of-God theologians" were right—if belief in God were on its way out—one would think that, after decades-long extermination campaigns, religion would certainly have been wiped out in Russia and China. Yet when the Soviet Union collapsed after more than seventy years of state atheism, what emerged strong from the ashes was belief in God. The Russian

Orthodox Church is again a leading force in the society, and there are many other active churches, mosques, and other religious groups. A similar scenario unfolded in China. In 1949, when Chairman Mao began his campaign to eradicate religion and especially Christianity, there were fewer than five million Christians in China. Today, there are far more than fifty million, even as Christians are still under pressure. These cases demonstrate that there is something deeply religious in the human spirit.

The Bible accounts for this in the opening story of creation, when it says that "God created human beings in God's image." (Genesis 1:27) There is much that can be said about what it means to be created "in the image of God," but the fundamental meaning is that *human beings are designed to be in a relationship with God*. Here is the one coherent explanation for why the ancients all believed in God—because there is in fact a Creator God who has placed in every human being a deep longing for God and an ability to connect with God.

Over time, as people reflected about their belief in God, they would come to see that this belief could be rationally grounded in a variety of ways. Those approaches toward establishing a rational basis for faith will be the subject of the next chapters. But the fundamental ground of religion is God, and the way that the human heart is drawn toward God. It is what is portrayed in Abraham, who encounters God, and lifts his heart in faith.

Moses said to God, "If I come to the Israelites and say to them, 'The God of your ancestors has sent me to you,' and they ask me, 'What is his name?' what shall I say to them?" God said to Moses, "I AM WHO I AM." He said further, "Thus you shall say to the Israelites, 'I AM has sent me to you.'" (Exodus 3:13-14)

Proving God

In the Vatican, in a large room, there is a famous painting by Raphael that depicts Plato and Aristotle. Aristotle has his hand stretched out, a reference to Aristotle's belief that human beings find truth by examining the world around them. Plato points up, a reference to his conviction that truth is discovered by looking upward to the pure realm of ideas. It is through Plato's approach that the first "proof" for God is conceived.

Ancient peoples long before Plato and Aristotle felt no need to prove God. The reality of God seemed obvious. This is particularly evident in the Biblical story. Throughout the sixty-six books of the Bible, there is no effort whatsoever to prove the existence of God. The Bible *declares* God. God in the Bible is not an idea to be proved but a reality to be encountered.

Nevertheless, as civilization advanced, and some people began to express questions about God, there was increasing motivation to think about rational arguments that would support the longstanding human belief in God. These arguments have come to be known as "proofs" for God. Most of these proofs have followed the course of Aristotle — looking at the elements of the natural world, and reasoning from evidence observed to the existence of God. But one approach uniquely follows Plato and begins with the idea of God itself. This is called the *ontological argument*, because it reasons from the very being (in Greek — *ontos*) of God.

It is a given that human beings have an idea of God, and have had this idea as far back as anyone can trace. Plato argued that the realm of ideas (or "forms" as he called them) is actually more real than the realm of the things that people observe in the world around them, since ideas have perfection and constancy, while the observable world is always flawed and in flux. For example, you have an idea of a circle, which is more perfect and true than any circular object that you will find in the world around you, since all natural "circles" are imperfect. The moon is full of craters, and even the sun — the most perfectly circular natural object observable from earth — bulges ever so slightly in the middle. Thinkers who follow Plato thus look for ultimate truth in the realm of ideas.

Is it possible that the very idea of God contains within itself the proof that God exists? This notion — that the *idea* of God itself could confirm the reality of God — is the heart of the ontological argument, which came to one of its most famous expressions in Anselm of Canterbury, who wrote his classic *Proslogion*, a discourse on the existence of God, in the eleventh century. He began with a simple, self-evident definition of God — *God is that, greater than which nothing can be conceived*. Everyone, Anselm noted, has this basic concept when they think of God, that God is the Ultimate, beyond which there can be nothing greater. But might this exist only as an idea in the mind, and not also in reality? Yet if God is only an idea in the mind, then there is something greater; for what exists in reality is greater than something which exists in the mind only. Therefore God must exist, in reality as well as in the mind, in order to be that, greater than which nothing can be conceived.[ii]

The genius of Anselm's argument is that it moves simply and inescapably from the idea of God to the conclusion that

God must exist. Yet from the moment *Proslogion* was written, not everyone was sure that this argument worked. Human beings entertain many imaginary ideas — ideas of unicorns, for example. Why cannot the idea of God — however it is conceived — be an idea like that? The answer, encapsulated in the ontological argument, is that the idea of God is fundamentally different from imaginary or theoretical ideas, because with regard to the idea of God, existence is inherent in the idea.

When people think of unicorns, they know that they are fanciful. But when people have thought of God, they have always thought of God as actual and existing. You can think of a unicorn without thinking of one being in your back yard; but you cannot think of God without also thinking of God as existing. In other words, in the idea of God, the existence of God is a necessary part of the idea. This line of reasoning was pursued especially by René Descartes, who put forth a significant restatement of the ontological argument in the seventeenth century. Like Plato and Anselm, Descartes looked for truth in what he called "clear and distinct ideas."

Descartes observed that when we have a clear and distinct idea of something, there are certain attributes that are necessarily a part of the thing conceived. He used the example of a triangle, which must have three angles adding up to 180 degrees, or a mountain, which must have an accompanying valley. Generally speaking, existence is not a necessary attribute of things. The fact that you can conceive of a mountain does not mean that there are any mountains in the world. But there are necessary attributes of things; if there is a mountain, it is absolutely certain that there must also be a valley; and if there is a triangle, it must have three angles.

In the case of God, existence is a necessary attribute. A "god" without existence is no god, just as a "triangle" without three angles is no triangle. The only way one can think of God is to also think of God existing. Therefore God must exist, since existence necessarily pertains to God. As Descartes put it, "From the fact that I cannot conceive God without existence, it follows that existence is inseparable from God."[iii]

When people have objected to the ontological arguments of Descartes or Anselm or others, the general approach is to try to find holes in the logic. The main objection is that existence is not an attribute, but only a way of saying that a thing described has a referent in the real world.[iv] Yet behind the swirl of logical debate, there is a basic reality at the core of the ontological argument—human beings throughout time have had a fundamental idea of God. Why?

The clearest explanation for the persistent appearance of the idea of God in human beings is that the idea refers to an actual Reality. Those who wish to deny the reality of God must therefore come up with some explanation for why people would have this idea of God if no God actually exists. This has proved difficult. In recent centuries, there has been a long series of attempts to offer a naturalistic explanation for why human beings have an idea of God. In the eighteenth century, David Hume argued that belief in God arose out of an effort by ancient humans to explain and control their ofttimes frightening world.[v] In the nineteenth century, Ludwig Feuerbach posited that the idea of God is a projection of the highest human aspirations and desires onto a cosmic grid.[vi] In the twentieth century, Sigmund Freud argued that belief in God arises out of the Oedipus complex and the need to deal with repressed guilt and fear.[vii] Today there are many other efforts to provide a naturalistic explanation of religion, which seek to trace the idea of God to psychological, sociological, or evolutionary causes. There is great divergence amongst these theories, even within the same thinker. Hume, Feuerbach, and Freud all made changes within the course of their lifetimes in their "explanations" of the idea of God. If there is anything consistent across all these theories, it is that they quite typically involve enormous assumptions, disregard actual research into religion, and are highly speculative.

A particularly glaring example of this is Freud's last major book on religion, *Moses and Monotheism*, in which he argued that Moses was actually an Egyptian whose monotheism was that of the pharaoh Akhenaten. But this Moses, Freud asserted, was killed by his followers, who subsequently viewed him as a tribal father figure, who recapitulated the ancient pattern of the father being killed by the sons — according to the Oedipus myth that dominated Freud's thinking. These followers, carrying repressed guilt, merged with another Midianite tribe to form the Jewish people, who thereafter carried a deep sense of guilt in their religion, and who invented the idea of a Messiah as a way of dealing with the long-repressed guilt that stemmed from the murder of father Moses. There is absolutely no evidence for any of this.

Freud's thesis now appears as a bizarre fabrication, constructed out of a series of utterly fanciful assumptions. Yet his approach illustrates a broader trend — those seeking to explain away religion have often been prone toward contrived arguments. Many of the naturalistic explanations for religion have sounded reasonable at the time — Freud's theories were based on his popular ideas about psychoanalysis — but they never stand up in the face of a serious study of the worldwide phenomenology of religion.

It is not so easy to conjure away the idea of God. As noted in the previous chapter, there is within human beings a deep and abiding sense of the Divine, which is so universal and so expansive across the millennia that it is not amenable to any easy explanation. Of course, one might suggest that the specific formulations of Anselm and Descartes were also a bit too simple and clever to comprehend the profound Mystery that is at the heart of religion. Yet for all the weaknesses of the "ontological argument," there is an accurate core perception at its center — human beings have a persistent and universal idea of God, which itself points to the reality of God.

Does this "prove" the existence of God? Interestingly enough, while the ontological argument is often put forth as the first of the so-called proofs for God, the nature of the argument calls into question the whole enterprise of "proving God." If God is the Ultimate — "that greater than which nothing can be conceived" — then God is far beyond human beings, and finally beyond human conception. Who therefore are human beings to *prove God*? God must be well beyond the grasp of the human mind.

This in fact is the picture of God that comes forth in the Biblical story. A prime example is the story of Moses, who encounters God in a mysteriously burning bush. When Moses attempts to learn the "name" of God — and thus to get some sort of handle on God — God declares, I AM. (Exodus 3:14) God is beyond human definition or comprehension. God is. Indeed it appears far too limiting to think of God as a particular being, no matter how perfect that being may be thought to be. God is Being itself; or as Paul Tillich famously put it, God is the Ground of Being (*der Grund des Seins*).[viii]

Thus any attempt to prove God — or disprove God — is as preposterous as an attempt to prove or disprove reality. The "proofs" for God are better understood as pointers to God — pieces of evidence that direct human beings to recognize the existence and nature of God. Subsequent chapters will examine those many layers of evidence. The evidence begins with the very idea of God, which — like the idea of a flower or the idea of love — would seem to reflect a Reality.

In the beginning God created the heavens and the earth. And the earth was without form and void, and darkness was upon the face of the deep, and the Spirit of God was moving over the face of the waters. Then God said, "Let there be light"; and there was light. And God saw that the light was good; and God separated the light from the darkness. God called the light Day, and the darkness Night. And there was evening and there was morning, the first day. (Genesis 1:1–5)

In the Beginning God

Why is there something rather than nothing? This is an age-old question. How can one account for the existence of the universe? Both Plato and Aristotle observed that everything that exists, or everything that happens, has a cause. When it rains, this is caused by clouds; but of course the clouds are caused by other physical events, and those events had a cause, and so on. Behind every observed effect there is a cause, which itself is the effect of a prior cause, in an endless chain of cause and effect. But, as Aristotle observed, the chain of causes cannot extend back infinitely, "for the series must start with something, since nothing can come from nothing."[ix] Obviously, at some point in the distant past, there must be a First Cause.

Thomas Aquinas built upon Aristotle and gave extensive consideration to this line of thought, which is now called the *cosmological argument* for the existence of God, since it points to the nature of the cosmos as a foundation for belief in God. Aquinas' basic point was that behind everything that exists in the cosmos, behind all the swirling suns and galaxies, there must be a First Mover, an Uncaused Cause — and this we call God.[x]

Moreover, the essence of God must be different from everything observed in nature, because with regard to every element in the cosmos, it is possible for a thing to be, or to not be. But, as Thomas Aquinas observed, "If everything can not be, then at one time there was nothing in existence. Yet if this were true, even now there would be nothing in existence. Therefore there must exist something the existence of which is necessary... which all speak of as God."[xi]

The cosmological argument has received many expressions,[xii] all of which observe that everything in the cosmos must depend for existence on Something which itself is not dependent. Sometimes people have tried to skirt around the cosmological argument by insisting that the universe "just is," but this simply leaves the question unanswered as to "why there is something rather than nothing." Moreover, as Thomas Aquinas pointed out, if things which have a possibility of "not being" are situated within infinite time, there will definitely be a time when things are not, which means there will no longer be anything, since the only thing that can come from nothing is nothing.

In recent years a few physicists have tried to answer that conundrum by suggesting that perhaps something *can* come from nothing. Stephen Hawking, in his 2010 book, *The Grand Design*, tried to argue that the universe could have spontaneously arisen through the action of gravity. He stated, "Because there is a law such as gravity, the universe can and will create itself from nothing." But gravity is not nothing; neither is the substance upon which gravity works. From where exactly did these physical laws and elements arise? Hawking had no explanation. A similar problem appears in Lawrence Krauss's 2012 book, *A Universe from Nothing*, in which he argued that the principles of quantum mechanics combined with the principles of relativity could result in space-time bubbles emerging out of nothing. Physicists have objected to the physics arguments in the book. But the fundamental flaw in the thesis, once again, is philosophical. Krauss does not actually argue that the universe comes from *nothing*, but that the universe comes out of quantum fields and laws of physics. But where did *they* originate? David

Albert, a Columbia University professor of philosophy who is also a physicist, summed up the philosophical critique of such an argument in a New York Times book review: "Where, for starters, are the laws of quantum mechanics themselves supposed to have come from?... The fundamental laws of [quantum field theory] take the form of rules concerning which arrangements of those fields are physically possible and which aren't, and rules connecting the arrangements of those fields at later times to their arrangements at earlier times, and so on — and they have nothing whatsoever to say on the subject of where those fields came from, or of why the world should have consisted of the particular kinds of fields it does, or of why it should have consisted of fields at all, or of why there should have been a world in the first place. Period. Case closed. End of story."[xiii] It continues to be impossible to explain how something came out of nothing — without reference to God.

In recent decades, the thrust of the cosmological argument has been developed in a further direction, as people have wondered not only why there is something rather than nothing, but why there is the particular something that exists rather than the many other possibilities that could have been. In this regard, a number of physicists have argued *for* the existence of God. An early case of this was Fred Hoyle, a self-professed atheist, who was doing research on stellar nucleosynthesis, the process by which elements are formed in stars. He observed that not much carbon should be produced by this process; and yet the universe is full of carbon — an intriguing fact, since carbon is the core building block for life. Hoyle calculated that so much carbon could be produced in stars only if there was a very specific "resonance" (energy level) and spin of the atoms involved, and this was extremely unlikely, given the range of possible values for the whole scenario. Yet, he found, the atomic values are at precisely the levels required. He called this a "monstrous coincidence." How is it, he thought, that carbon just happens to have this very improbable set of properties that are exactly what is needed for a universe that will sustain life? Hoyle concluded, "Would you not say to yourself, 'Some super-calculating intellect must have designed the properties of the carbon atom, otherwise the chance of my finding such an atom through the blind forces of nature would be utterly minuscule.' A common sense interpretation of the facts suggests that a superintellect has monkeyed with physics, as well as with chemistry and biology, and that there are no blind forces worth speaking about in nature. The numbers one calculates from the facts seem to me so overwhelming as to put this conclusion almost beyond question."[xiv]

Hoyle thus became one of many physicists to observe a kind of remarkable "Goldilocks effect" in the universe as a whole—the physics are "just right" to produce a universe that will support life. For example, the astronomer Owen Gingerich pointed out that if the energy of the Big Bang had been a little less, the universe would have fallen back on itself long before life could appear; but if the energy had been a little more, the density of the rapidly expanding universe would have dropped too quickly for stars or galaxies to form. The "bang" at the beginning was set just right.[xv] Stephen Hawking made a similar observation when looking at the subatomic world. He said, "The laws of science, as we know them at present, contain many fundamental numbers, like the size of the electric charge of the electron and the ratio of the masses of the proton and the electron... The remarkable fact is that the values of these numbers seem to have been very finely adjusted to make possible the development of life."[xvi] The physicist Paul Davies likewise noted that a whole host of physical properties have a "just right" setting. He put it this way:

"Life as we know it depends very sensitively on the form of the laws of physics and on some seemingly fortuitous accidents in the actual values that nature has chosen for various particle masses, force strengths, and so on. If we could play God, and set values for these natural quantities at whim by twiddling a set of knobs, we would find that almost all knob settings would render the universe uninhabitable."[xvii]

The universe appears to be finely tuned, so as to be conducive to life. As Owen Gingerich observed, "Many details are so extraordinarily right that it seems the universe has been expressly designed for human life."[xviii] Of course, this is exactly what the Bible declares. The opening verses of Genesis proclaim that God created the world with the intent that it would have life, at the pinnacle of which would be human beings. Science has made clear that such a life-sustaining universe, if it were to arise by pure chance, would be extravagantly unlikely. But this is exactly the universe we have. Thus the universe has every appearance of being what the Bible describes—a universe intentionally produced by a Divine Creator.

How else can one account for the amazingly fortuitous conjunction of all the physical laws and values necessary for a world that is ideal for human life? One possibility, of course, is that the human race just got lucky. In the cosmic role of the dice, all the right numbers just happened to come up. Yet the number of factors requiring a "just right" setting is so extravagantly enormous that *luck* is scarcely a tenable theory to account for the universe!

In recent years, some scientists, recognizing the extreme unlikelihood of our universe as it is, have tried to account for this Goldilocks universe by suggesting that there are an infinite number of universes, with infinite arrangements of physical values. If that is the case, then there are universes with all possible structures, so that this universe is simply the one with all the right values for life. Stephen Hawking appealed to this "multiverse" idea in his book, *The Grand Design*, to account for that fact that, as his partner Thomas Hertog later put it, "The laws of nature we observe in our universe appear to be very special, delicate, in a sense."[xix] Such "special" laws can arise by chance only if there are an infinite number of chances (universes) for them to appear!

But the multiverse theory was always highly conjectural and had no evidence to support it. At the end of his life, in his last scientific paper, Stephen Hawking refuted the concept of infinite random universes, suggesting instead that the entire cosmos must be governed by the same fundamental physical laws.[xx] But this leaves open the basic question that he posed in *The Grand Design*; as he said: "Our universe and its laws appear to have a design that both is tailor-made to support us and, if we are to exist, leaves little room for alteration. That is not easily explained, and raises the natural question of why it is that way."[xxi]

Why is it this way? How does one account for this "just right" universe? There is a principle in philosophy known as Occam's razor, named after the fourteenth century logician William of Ockham, which says that when choosing between a simple and direct solution to a problem versus a highly convoluted one, the simple solution is most likely correct. The most straightforward explanation for the fact that the universe appears to be fine-tuned for human life is that the universe has in fact been finely tuned by God.

The Bible begins, "In the beginning God created the heavens and the earth. And the earth was without form and void, and darkness was upon the face of the deep, and the Spirit of God was moving over the face of the waters. And God said, 'Let there be light.' And there was light." (Genesis 1:1–3)

In poetic language, the Bible describes exactly what science now describes in the Big Bang. The universe was without form and void. There was darkness. And then, in a moment, there was a burst of light. It is rather remarkable that the Bible speaks of light bursting forth before there was a sun. But this is exactly what happens in the Big Bang. Out of nothingness comes light, and all of creation.

A further intriguing feature of Genesis' description of the beginning of creation is the statement that God created "evening and morning, the first day." (Genesis 1:5) In other words, God created time—which physicists also tell us began with the Big Bang.

But what stands before the Big Bang? What set all things in motion, and what established the physical parameters that would produce the incredible universe that human beings now occupy and perceive? Whatever stands before the Big Bang must be beyond space and time, but must also possess infinite wisdom, to produce the incredible universe that now exists. That is a rather perfect description of God.

More than two millennia after Aristotle, and nearly nine hundred years after Thomas Aquinas, the cosmological "proof" of God stands. The only way to truly account for this universe is to point to God—the Source of all that is.

Bless the Lord, O my soul. O Lord my God, you are very great. You are clothed with honor and majesty, wrapped in light as with a garment. You stretch out the heavens like a tent, you set the beams of your chambers on the waters, you make the clouds your chariot, you ride on the wings of the wind, you make the winds your messengers, fire and flame your ministers. You set the earth on its foundations, so that it shall never be shaken. You cover it with the deep as with a garment; the waters stood above the mountains. At your rebuke they flee; at the sound of your thunder they take to flight. They rose up to the mountains, ran down to the valleys to the place that you appointed for them. You set a boundary that they may not pass, so that they might not again cover the earth. You make springs gush forth in the valleys; they flow between the hills, giving drink to every wild animal; the wild donkeys quench their thirst. By the streams the birds of the air have their habitation; they sing among the branches. From your lofty abode you water the mountains; the earth is satisfied with the fruit of your work. You cause the grass to grow for the cattle, and plants for people to use, to bring forth food from the earth, and wine to gladden the human heart, oil to make the face shine, and bread to strengthen the human heart. The trees of the Lord are watered abundantly, the cedars of Lebanon that he planted. In them the birds build their nests; the stork has its home in the fir trees. The high mountains are for the wild goats; the rocks are a refuge for the badgers. You have made the moon to mark the seasons; the sun knows its time for setting. You make darkness, and it is night, when all the animals of the forest come creeping out. The young lions roar for their prey, seeking their food from God. When the sun rises, they withdraw and lie down in their dens. People go out to their work and to their labor until the evening.

O Lord, how manifold are your works! In wisdom you have made them all; the earth is full of your creatures. (Psalm 104:1–14)

The Artistry of God

Albert Einstein, in an interview with G. S. Viereck, once remarked, "We are in the position of a little child entering a huge library filled with books in many different languages. The child knows someone must have written those books. It does not know how. The child dimly suspects a mysterious order in the arrangement of the books..."xxii There is an extraordinary complexity, order, and design in the universe. Human beings, like the child in that library, have long surmised that there must be an intelligent Power responsible for it all.

William Paley famously imagined walking across an English heath and stumbling upon a watch lying on the ground. From where did the watch come? It would be no answer at all to suggest that the watch had just always been there, or that it assembled itself by chance. From the elaborate complexity of the watch, with all the minute pieces working in conjunction for the purpose of tracking time, it is obvious that there must have been a Watchmaker.xxiii

Both Paley and Einstein give expression to what is now called the *teleological argument* for the existence of God—from the Greek word *telos*, meaning end or goal or purpose. The argument points out what a masterful construction the universe is, and concludes that it must have been designed on purpose.

25

The teleological argument and the cosmological argument are similar and overlap somewhat, in that both begin with the observed world and reason from it to the necessary existence of God. The difference between the two is that whereas the cosmological approach argues from *contingency* — that all that is depends ultimately upon a First Cause, or Prime Mover — the teleological approach argues from *design* — that the incredible order, complexity, and beauty of the universe must be the result of a Master Designer.

In the Bible, the cosmological argument is reflected in the opening of Genesis, which declares that God is the source of all that is. The teleological argument is reflected especially in the creation psalms — several Psalms that include a meditation on the glory of the universe. Psalm 19 exults, "The heavens declare the glory of God, and the sky proclaims God's handiwork." (Psalm 19:1) The "heavens" (Hebrew — הַשָּׁמַיִם *hashamayim*) refer to the sun and moon and stars. The Psalmist beholds the wonder of the cosmos, and recognizes that it is the "handiwork" of God. Another creation psalm turns further attention towards smaller things on earth. Psalm 104, the longest of the creation psalms, speaks of one sort of animal after another and notes how marvelous each one is and how they all fit within a magnificent world. The Psalm proclaims, "O Lord, how manifold are Your works! In wisdom You have made them all." (Psalm 104:14) These psalms observe the marvelous structure of the world and the amazing diversity of its creatures and see that it is all the artistry of God.

Today, of course, some people want to argue that the theory of evolution contradicts belief in God as Creator. But in fact, there is no inherent conflict between the idea of evolution and the idea of God as Designer. The problem is that people often have too small an idea of what is meant by *design*.

When people have thought of God as designer or creator, they often have had in mind a very simple image of the craftsman — like the ancient potter, who designs and builds each pot. If there are to be different sorts of pots, the potter must

The Artistry of God

design and specifically make each one. This is the basic view of God in the idea of *creationism*, which suggests that God must have designed and crafted every star and every sort of living thing on earth.

But if God is God—if God is, as noted in a previous chapter, "that greater than which nothing can be conceived"—then this idea of God as designer is far too small. Which is greater: a God who, like the potter, must directly crank out every thing that is, or a God who creates structures—substances and natural laws and energy fields and principles of genetics—which themselves produce an endless array of new things? A God who is truly God will go far beyond the human craftsman to *create creativity*—a universe in which systems of creativity are actually built into the very fabric of things, so that the universe endlessly spawns new works. If God creates creativity, then the mechanisms of evolution are precisely what one should expect; for evolution describes a biological framework that is designed to endlessly and expansively produce new adaptations and life forms. Surely this is superior to a system in which a divine creator must directly fashion every new thing. The fact that God's approach is to create creativity is abundantly evident in the pinnacle of creation—human beings, who have been endowed with the highest sort of creativity in nature, in being able to intentionally create new things. A full view of God as Creator will recognize that God has not simply created static things, but rather God has created engines of creativity—quantum mechanics in the realm of physics and the mechanisms of evolution in the realm of biology and human beings at the summit of it all—so that the elements of the universe are not just created but themselves become a part of a creative process.

With this understanding of design, the idea of evolution is not only compatible with the idea of God as Designer, but it is the necessary corollary of it; for what finally must be the approach of a God who is truly the Intelligent Designer? Is the Intelligent Designer a God who creates by individually designing every feature of every creature that ever existed, and who constantly tweaks each species as the environment changes, so that God is cranking out endless designs through the ages, like an architect's office that is furiously sending out blueprints? Or is the Intelligent Designer a God who creates life in such a fashion that it has creativity built into it, so that life forms will automatically develop into new forms, so that once started there will be an endless and fantastic explosion of new life forms that will constantly adjust to the surroundings? Surely the latter is the intelligent design—a world that has a fundamental mechanism of creativity built into it, a mechanism that human beings have discovered and now call evolution.

When the Bible speaks of God as creator, it declares *that* God creates, and never gets into detail as to *how* God creates. The creation is described in grand poetry, in Genesis 1 and in the creation psalms. Nevertheless, there are interesting parallels between the poetic picture in the first chapter of Genesis and the basic outline of the evolutionary process on planet earth. The "six days of creation" in Genesis—a poetic statement never meant to be taken literally!—portray a process of progressive development over time, from the physical earth through more and more complex life forms and finally to the appearance of humanity. Moreover, it is clear that the creative power of God works through the stuff of the earth. Genesis 1:20 declares, "And God said, 'Let the waters bring forth swarms of living creatures.'" Genesis 1:24 continues, "Let the earth bring forth living creatures of every kind." Finally, in the creation of humanity, it is said, "God formed humankind from the dust of the ground." (Genesis 2:7) There is an understanding that God creates, not by means of an instantaneous zap from heaven, but through a progressive process that utilizes the materials and developing structures in the natural world.

Thus it makes sense to recognize God as Designer, and the science of evolution as the description of how the design unfolds in the development of life forms. Of course, there are those who want to argue that God can be left out of this picture and that everything can be explained purely as the result of mechanistic forces operating by chance. It is true that chance is an *operating principle* in the process of evolution, as the chance combination and mutation of genes will produce endless new possibilities for life. But chance does not suffice as an *explanatory principle* for the world. It was already observed, in the previous chapter, that chance cannot account for the extraordinary arrangements of natural laws in the physical universe; and likewise chance alone cannot account for the extraordinary nature of the abundant living world on planet earth.

Many people have observed that the biological world is so complex, so intricate, so interconnected and interdependent that it simply cannot be explained as being the result of pure chance. Fred Hoyle stated flatly, "As biochemists discover more and more about the awesome complexity of life, it is apparent that the chances of it originating by accident are so minute that they can be completely ruled out. Life cannot have arisen by chance."[xxiv] He went on to compare "the chance of obtaining even a single functioning protein by chance combination of amino acids to a star system full of blind men solving Rubik's Cube simultaneously."[xxv] But there is not only a serious problem in trying to explain the physical structures of the universe as being the result of pure chance. There is an even bigger problem that is revealed by the teleological argument as it shines light on the *artistry* of the world.

When human beings behold the world, their primary response is that of wonder, as they are struck by the magnificence of the natural world. This is the core sentiment at the heart of Psalm 104. But why is this so — that when people look at nature, they marvel at its beauty? If human beings are simply the result of cold, mechanistic processes of chance and survival, why would they even have a concept of beauty, and why would they feel a sense of joy and awe in looking at the surrounding world?

Why do people flock to national parks such as Arches or Bryce Canyon in order to look at hunks of rock? Why would they see a rock arch or pillar as something wonderful and amazing and inspiring? If this is just a material universe, and human beings are merely the result of mechanistic forces of chance and survival, then they should have no interest in a piece of rock, unless perhaps it could be used to build some shelter. Certainly there would be no reason to experience a rock formation or a canyon as *beautiful*. An appreciation for the form of a particular rock does absolutely nothing to enhance one's survival; in fact, if humans are just material beings geared for survival, they ought to be repulsed by an expanse of rocky desert because it is not a good place to survive.

Why do people go to great effort to engage in snorkeling or scuba diving, in order to look at coral and pretty fish? If human beings are simply material creatures who developed out of a dog eat dog struggle for survival, they should have no interest in looking at fish. They should just want to eat them.

What moves people to pause in a wintery landscape and gaze with wonder at the expanse of snow and trees? Again, if there nothing spiritual about human beings, if they are only the physical result of chemical processes, then they ought to be concerned for nothing more than getting out of the cold. Why do people gaze enraptured at flowers and sunsets and waves crashing on a beach? If this is a purely material universe, none of this makes any sense.

The fundamental human experience of the natural world is that it is a marvelous expanse of spiritually moving artistry. It only makes sense when one recognizes that there is an Artist behind it all. Human beings throughout the ages, as they have gazed upon the earth, have sensed that they were gazing at the brushstrokes of God.

In recent years, of course, human beings have come to understand more and more about how those brushstrokes happened. Scientists understand how a rock arch is formed by the action of wind, blowing sand, and rain, how different species of fish have developed, how weather patterns create and drop snow, and how flowers grow and sunsets form. But the fact that one understands how an artist created an artwork — how the paints were mixed and how the brushstrokes were applied — does nothing to diminish one's appreciation for the artist. In fact, you may appreciate the artist all the more when you understand the complexity of the processes used. Likewise, the fact that human beings now can understand forces in geology and biology and astronomy need not diminish appreciation for the divine artist who used those processes to shape the universe. Indeed many scientists today have a greater appreciation for God precisely because they understand the extraordinary processes that underlie all that they see.

In the end, the *artistic design* of the natural world — not only its intricate complexity but even more its beauty — points to the reality of the Designer. Such artistry has no explanation, unless there is an Artist, who has given to human beings the ability to appreciate and enjoy the wonder of it all. A full consideration of the marvelous glory of the universe thus leads inescapably to the recognition that God is the Creator behind all that is. St. Bonaventure summed it up well in these words: "Whoever, therefore, is not enlightened by such splendor of created things is blind; whoever is not awakened by such outcries is deaf; whoever does not praise God because of all these effects is dumb; whoever does not discover the First Principle from such signs is a fool. Therefore, open your eyes, alert the ears of your spirit, open your lips and apply your heart so that in all of creation you may see, hear, praise, love and worship, glorify and honor your God."[xxvi]

O give thanks to the Lord, for God is good. God's steadfast love endures forever. (Psalm 136:1)

Good and upright is the Lord. Therefore God instructs sinners in the way, and leads the humble in what is right. (Psalm 25:8–9)

Let them turn away from evil and do good. (I Peter 3:11)

God Is Good

Why do you think that some actions are good or right and some actions are wrong or bad? People universally have a sense of morality, but why is this so? Wild animals have no such moral sense. Consider the groundhogs or rabbits who eat up your garden; they have no concept of right or wrong, of goodness or evil. They simply do what is necessary to survive. Why then do human beings have this idea of "the good"? In the idea of right and wrong, people act as though there is a moral Authority, who is the source of what is good.

Sometimes it is argued that people in their moral thinking are just following cultural patterns. Your ideas of right and wrong, in this view, would stem simply from your family or your society. But if that is the case, then you would think that people in very different places and times would have very different ideas about right and wrong, and some people would have no such ideas at all.

Yet in fact, human beings in all times and places have not only had a basic idea of "the good" — that certain kinds of actions are morally right and the opposing actions are morally wrong — but the specific ideas of what is right or wrong are remarkably similar across every culture. For people in every place, stealing is wrong, untruthfulness is wrong, and murder is wrong, while generosity is good, honesty is good, and loving-kindness is good. Sometimes these values are applied only to one's own group—so that it is considered perfectly OK to kill and steal from the tribe over the hill—but at least within one's own tribe or clan, there is an idea that there is a basic "moral law"; and this moral law, in its broad scope, has been universal across the globe and across the millennia.

One example of this is the fact that there is some form of the "Golden Rule" in every major religion. In Hinduism there is the teaching, "Treat others as you treat yourself."[xxvii] In Zoroastrianism there is the rule, "Whatever is disagreeable to yourself do not do unto others."[xxviii] Buddhism teaches, "Hurt not others in ways that you yourself would find hurtful."[xxix] Confucianism has the teaching, "What you do not wish for yourself, do not do to others."[xxx] The Greek philosopher Isocrates, expressing the theme in Greek ethics, said, "Do not do to others that which angers you when they do it to you."[xxxi] The list goes on. The Bible expresses this principle in positive terms, in Leviticus 19:18, which says, "Love your neighbor as yourself," and in the teaching of Jesus, who brought the "Golden Rule" to its clearest positive statement when he said, "Do unto others as you would have them do unto you." (Matthew 7:12)

This kind of consistency can be found across numerous moral teachings in all different cultures. There seems to be a kind of Universal Moral Law—a basic concept of what is morally right and wrong that is found in all human beings. From where does this come? Why would people in disconnected cultures have the same basic moral values? There must be a common Source of morality.

Moreover, why do people universally have the idea that certain values are *objectively* good—that is, certain actions are "good" not because of a cultural or personal preference but because these actions are just inherently good. For example, to treat others with kindness, the moral value that is at the heart of the Golden Rule, is considered by everyone everywhere to be objectively good. It is not a value that is debatable or open to question, as though treating people with cruelty might be just as good a value. People universally have a sense that everyone ought to treat others with kindness, even if they don't feel like it or fall short of the value. But if there is objective morality—if what is good or evil is not a matter of subjective preference but is given by some immutable moral law—then there must be an ultimate principle or force for Goodness in the universe, which establishes that moral law and imparts a corresponding sense of morality to human beings. In short, the existence of a Universal Moral Law points to the necessary existence of God.

This basic line of argument, which reasons from human morality to the conclusion that there must be a God who is the source of that morality, is called the *moral argument* for the existence of God. Historically, the argument came to particular expression in Immanual Kant, who observed that human beings strive for a *summum bonum*—the greatest good—and that the only way to account for this drive for ultimate goodness is by acknowledging the existence of God.[xxxii] The moral argument has been further developed by many thinkers such as Hastings Rashdall[xxxiii] and C. S. Lewis.[xxxiv]

Biblically, the moral argument is strongly represented throughout the Scriptures. The Old Testament repeatedly declares that God is good (Psalm 136:1; Psalm 100:5) and that God imparts goodness to human beings. Psalm 25, for example, declares, "Good and upright is the Lord; therefore God instructs sinners [those who otherwise would not be good] in the way, and leads the humble in what is right." (Psalm 25:8–9) The Bible goes on to speak of God providing moral instruction in many forms—giving the commandments, for example, in Old Testament times, and giving moral inspiration through Jesus' teachings and through New Testament writings such as I Peter, which admonishes its readers to "turn away from evil and do good." (I Peter 3:11) Moreover, there is an understanding, expressed especially in Romans chapter one, that God has given to everyone a basic awareness of what is true and good, so that, as Paul says, "they are without excuse" (Romans 1:20) if they do wrong, because everyone has an innate, God-given sense of morality.

Today, of course, some people will say that they can be good without God, that belief in God is not necessary for morality. But the moral argument is not that people have to believe in God in order to be moral. It is rather that the Spirit of God is the source of the basic sense of morality that exists in all human beings, whether they believe in God or not. The fact that some individuals can follow moral principles without affirming belief in God does nothing to undercut the core insight of the moral argument — that there is an objective, universal idea of morality across all human beings.

It is very interesting that the person who says, "I can be good without God," will still insist that there are certain things that are objectively right or wrong — that slaughtering innocent people is "wrong," for example, and that helping the needy is "good." But this thinking plays right into the moral argument, because why in fact is it wrong to slaughter innocent people? If there is no God, if human beings are just material creatures in a survival-of-the-fittest universe, then there is no reason to claim that there is something wrong with slaughtering innocent people. The only way to claim that there are objective moral values is to affirm that there is an Ultimate Moral Authority — namely, God.

The essence of the moral argument is that the nature of human morality requires that there is a spiritual Source of that morality. This is precisely what the Bible proclaims, as it declares that God is good, and that the reason that human beings have an idea of the good, and a desire to do the good, is because of the working of God.

Those who wish to deny God must therefore come up with some way to account for the kind of morality that is observed in human beings without reference to God. One line of argument that is commonly put forth is to suggest that moral values are simply the result of practical measures to ensure that a community can function. Nothing works very well if everyone is dishonest, for example, and thus honesty becomes a generally approved value. In this scenario, human "values" are essentially self-serving, bringing benefit to oneself. People will practice the value of politeness, for example, because it generally moves other people to be polite in return.

But this line of argument does not explain morality. It explains civility — the customs that people adopt to function nicely with each other. Morality goes much further into areas that are not self-serving at all. The highest moral behavior is the practice of *altruism* — the willingness to sacrifice one's own interests to bring benefit to others. Altruism is celebrated across human cultures as the pinnacle of morally good behavior. But if there is no God, and human beings are simply the result of a dog eat dog struggle for survival, then altruism makes no sense at all. Human beings should not even consider sacrificing themselves for the sake of others; they should want only to dominate others.

In recent years, some atheists have tried to counter this problem by arguing that natural selection would have worked in favor of altruism, in that altruism would advance the "gene pool" in which the altruistic individual was situated. The behavior of sacrificing self for the sake of the colony would advance the colony and thus the genes that supported altruistic behavior. This actually does quite nicely explain the kind of apparent "altruism" that one observes among animals — the fact that parent animals will put themselves at risk to defend their young, for example, or that worker bees or ants will sacrifice themselves for the sake of the colony. But the argument that altruism in the clan advances the clan — while it explains the apparent altruism in animals — does not at all explain the sort of altruism that one observes in human beings, which is of an entirely different order; because the highest form of altruism among people is to give oneself for the sake of those *beyond* one's own circle. The belief that it is good to help the stranger, and to show care to the outsider, is found across world religions and comes to its peak expression in Jesus, who taught people to "love their enemy" and who sacrificed his own life for the sake of those who hated and opposed him.

If human beings are the result only of a struggle for the survival of the fittest, then the kind of values exhibited by Jesus should make no sense to anyone. In a godless, mechanistic universe, everyone should just be propelled by a basic concern for self and a drive to triumph over the other. It should not be a value that the strong should help the weak; in a survival-of-the fittest world, the only reasonable course is for the strong to eliminate the weak! It should not be a value that anyone would be shown mercy; and it should seem absolutely preposterous to "love one's enemy." Why then do people universally recognize Jesus as the embodiment of what is supremely good? Even those who do not affirm that Jesus is the Son of God will agree that he displayed the most praiseworthy values in helping the weak, in showing mercy, and in being willing to sacrifice the self, even for the outsider. There is no explanation for why people would affirm such values unless they are inspired by a transcendent source of morality, namely God.

In the end, human morality—the universal sense that there is an objective moral law, which calls people beyond themselves to live by higher values—points to the necessary existence of an ultimate Lawgiver. What the Bible affirms is what makes sense: the human moral awareness, which far transcends anything in the natural world, comes from God, who has created human beings in God's image, which is why the goodness of God is now reflected in the human heart.

It will always be possible for people to be good or to do good without believing in God. All they have to do is to follow the prompting of the inner moral conscience that God has given to them, and ride the wave of the general moral awareness in the culture around them. It will also always be possible for people to choose against goodness and do evil, but in that case their actions will be recognized as evil by all the people around them. The central question, which is at the core of the moral argument, is the question as to the source of that moral sense, which is within all human beings and across every culture. The only coherent explanation for the human idea of the Good is what the Bible declares: that God is Good, and God has imparted a basic moral consciousness to every human being — and a basic calling, to not only know the good, but to do it.

Jacob left Beer-sheba and went toward Haran. He came to a certain place and stayed there for the night, because the sun had set. Taking one of the stones of the place, he put it under his head and lay down in that place. And he dreamed that there was a ladder set up on the earth, the top of it reaching to heaven; and the angels of God were ascending and descending on it. And the Lord stood beside him and said, "I am the Lord, the God of Abraham your father and the God of Isaac; the land on which you lie I will give to you and to your offspring; and your offspring shall be like the dust of the earth, and you shall spread abroad to the west and to the east and to the north and to the south; and all the families of the earth shall be blessed in you and in your offspring. Know that I am with you and will keep you wherever you go, and will bring you back to this land; for I will not leave you until I have done what I have promised you." Then Jacob woke from his sleep and said, "Surely the Lord is in this place—and I did not know it!" And he was afraid, and said, "How awesome is this place! This is none other than the house of God, and this is the gate of heaven."

So Jacob rose early in the morning, and he took the stone that he had put under his head and set it up for a pillar and poured oil on the top of it. He called that place Bethel ["house of God"] but the name of the city was Luz at the first. Then Jacob made a vow, saying, "If God will be with me, and will keep me in this way that I go, and will give me bread to eat and clothing to wear, so that I come again to my father's house in peace, then the Lord shall be my God, and this stone, which I have set up for a pillar, shall be God's house; and of all that you give me I will surely give one-tenth to you." (Genesis 28:1–22)

The Spirit Bears Witness Within Us

Have you had an experience of the presence of God? Many people would say "yes" to that question. It is typical for believers to have had some kind of experience of the nearness or working of God. As Paul said in Romans, "The Spirit bears witness with our spirit that we are children of God." (Romans 8:16)

For some people who have had a deep experience of God, no "proof" for God is necessary. You don't need to prove the existence of Someone you have met. The classic "proofs for God" are designed for people who are skeptics, or who may have sensed the reality of God, but still have doubts.

With regard to those who have felt no experience of God, it may seem impossible to make an argument for God's existence based on religious experience; but it is in fact to the doubters that the *argument from religious experience* is directed, for this argument is based, not so much on one's own personal religious experience, but on the broad experience of humanity. It was noted in the first chapter that every human culture has been religious; and religion has been grounded not on abstract theological concepts but on a deep human awareness of the Divine. In every place and time, people have claimed to have experienced on some level a spiritual Power, a divine Presence.

If there is no God, how can one explain the fact that countless people say they have experienced God? Perhaps one could counter by observing that people have claimed to have experienced other things that are not actually real. People claim to have sighted UFOs, or claim to have seen Bigfoot. But such claims are quite different from religious claims to have experienced God, because they are very limited in both space and time. Supposed sightings of UFOs only began with the dawn of the space age, and the sightings of Bigfoot only began after rumors emerged of some creature in the northwest. These claims are clearly contingent upon a certain culture, region, and point in time.

But the experience of God can be found in every culture, in every corner of the world, for as far back in time as one can research. If God does not exist, then billions of people from countless societies across the millennia have all been deluded, because they all claimed to have experienced God. The commonality of religious experience through the ages is strong evidence that people are in fact experiencing a Reality.

Sometimes people will try to argue that the experience of God is not in fact so common to humanity because there are many differences between religions, and thus people must be having different experiences. But in fact the opposite is the case. It is true that there are many differences between religions in doctrine and practice. But the more one penetrates beneath doctrine and traditions to the level of experience, the more commonality there is among religions. Look at the mystical writings in any religion — the writings of those who have had a deep experience of the Divine — and you will find a remarkable similarity in the descriptions of what is experienced. Those who study the phenomenology of religion will often observe that while religions have significant differences in doctrines, they are more similar on the level of story and symbol, and they become very similar on the level of experience. Why would this be? The only coherent explanation is that all religions on a deep level are connecting with the same reality of God.

A further indication of the authenticity of religious experience is the effect it produces. People who report a powerful religious experience are changed and typically motivated thereafter to great devotion and often self-sacrifice. A prime example in the Biblical story is the apostle Paul, whose experience of the Risen Christ reversed the course of his life and motivated him to devote the rest of his life, at great sacrifice, to the spread of the gospel. How can an experience have such a powerful effect unless it is the experience of something Real?

If so many people at so many places and times say that they have perceived Something, and if their lives show real effects of that experience, it follows that that Something — namely God — actually exists.

At the same time, if religious experience is fundamentally encounter with God, it makes sense that just as human encounters between people will occur in many different ways, so the religious experience will likely take many different shapes and forms; and this is in fact the case. Sometimes people have an intense experience of an encounter with God. In the Bible there are a number of stories of such encounters, from the story of Moses at the burning bush to the story of Paul on the Damascus road. Today such intense experiences can range from near death experiences to dramatic conversion experiences, when people have a particular moment when they have an overwhelming sense of the gracious presence of God. John Wesley, founder of the Methodist movement, had such an experience on Aldersgate Street in London on May 24, 1738. He was attending a religious gathering, when suddenly, he said, he "felt his heart strangely warmed" by the merciful presence of Christ. That personal experience of the grace of Christ became the pivotal moment in his faith journey, which transformed his ministry. People who have such intense experiences can typically name the day and the hour.

Other times religious experience is more subtle and may actually include an expanse of varied experiences over time. Sometimes when people are out in nature, taking a walk through the woods, or standing on a shore looking over the water, they have a sense of Something More — an awareness that there is a greater Power behind all that is seen. People can have a similar kind of experience in worship, perhaps during a particular song, or in a moment of silence, when they sense the nearness of God. Sometimes religious experience comes through an intentional religious practice, such as prayer; other times it hits people unexpectedly. Religious experience can also take the form of an experience of guidance or help at a moment of need. But as varied as religious experiences can be, there is a common element at the core of them all — a sense of an Ultimate Reality, who, although infinite, is immediately at hand.

Historically, the argument from religious experience gained particular emphasis during the period of Romanticism, which, following the Enlightenment's focus on Reason, put renewed accent on the role of feeling and intuition in human knowing. Friedrich Schleiermacher, for example, writing in the early nineteenth century, argued that the essence of religion is to be found in inward feeling, whereby human beings have a sense of absolute dependence and a corresponding consciousness of God.[xxxv] Such religious feelings, he contended, are a response to an actual divine Reality. Interest in the nature of religious experience continued to grow in many quarters and reached a kind of crescendo at the turn of the twentieth century in William James' *Varieties of Religious Experience*.[xxxvi] James' writing was burdened by some naturalistic assumptions that he made — assumptions common to his own age — but the extended focus of many thinkers on religious experience served finally to illuminate how religious experience can be a window into the working of God.

In the Bible, one of the most memorable stories about spiritual experience is that of Jacob's ladder. The story is especially illuminating, as it portrays key elements that have been common to religious experience throughout the ages.

In the book of Genesis, beginning in chapter 25, Jacob appears as a young man who is a rascal and not at all religious. In his desire to get ahead in life, he swindles his brother Esau on two occasions — in order to get Esau's share of the family inheritance. Jacob thereby connects perfectly with the common values of contemporary culture, where many people are primarily concerned with self-advancement, and religion is not a priority.

But Jacob's escapades infuriate his brother Esau, who sets about to take Jacob's life. Jacob is forced to flee to seek refuge with his distant uncle Laban. Genesis 28 describes how Jacob, running for his life, finds a spot to lie down for the night. He uses a rock for pillow. It is a poignant illustration of being in a very difficult place.

There Jacob has a dream or a vision in which he sees a ladder extending from earth to heaven, and angels are ascending and descending on it. The ladder signifies a direct connection between God and humanity. The experience culminates with Jacob sensing that God is standing beside him and saying to him, "Know that I am with you and will keep you wherever you go." (Genesis 28:15) This is the heart of religious experience — a sense of the presence of God.

It is significant that this experience happened when Jacob was in distress, in a lonely and insecure place. Intense religious experiences often occur when life is in some way disrupted. When people are confronted by their limitations and their mortality, and the future appears opaque, that very disruption of life's comfort zones can sometimes open the door to the experience of Something More. In the case of Jacob, it was a low point in life that became precisely the place where he had a high point of religious experience. He would subsequently name the place, Bethel, which means "house of God."

Jacob's initial response to this divine encounter was one of fear and awe. "He was afraid," reports Genesis, "and said, 'How awesome is this place.'" (Genesis 28:17) This is precisely the sort of experience discussed in chapter one. Jacob encountered the *mysterium tremendum et fascinans* — the Divine Mystery that is both fearsome and yet also gracious and attracting — and it provoked in him a deep sense of reverence and awe.

This led to Jacob's next response, which was that of worship. Genesis reports that "Jacob took the stone that he had put under his head and set it up for a pillar and poured oil on the top of it." (Genesis 28:18) This describes a very ancient form of creating a sanctuary or place of worship. The erected stone pillar calls to mind other ancient sanctuaries with pillars such as Stonehenge or Göbekli Tepe, and there are many examples of individual pillars like this in the ancient near east. The anointing of the pillar with oil was an act of consecrating it for worship.[xxxvii]

This act of worship led finally to a commitment to moral change. It is remarkable to read of how grasping, self-centered Jacob made a vow in which he said, "Of all that God gives me I will surely give one-tenth to God." (Genesis 28:22) This is an early statement of the tithe — the Biblical practice of giving ten percent of one's annual income to God. What would move Jacob, who up to this point had been nothing but a self-focused rascal, to suddenly resolve to give ten percent to God? It is an illustration of how an authentic encounter with God changes people's behavior and priorities, moving people from self-centeredness toward a life of giving.

It must be noted that Jacob at this point was still a long way from moral perfection. There was a kind of crass bargaining that was evident in his commitment to God — "If you help me and bless me," he said, "I will give to you." Subsequent stories of Jacob show that he still had a lot of spiritual maturing to do. It is frequently the case that an experience of God does not produce instant holiness! Yet religious experience very often produces a long-term moral effect, inspiring people to embark into a life of growing moral character and goodness — something one sees in Jacob.

The story of Jacob's ladder encapsulates the major elements that can be found in religious experiences across the centuries and across the globe. Not everyone sees a ladder, of course. Religious experiences take many different forms. But religious experiences of all types regularly contain these core elements: the sense of the presence of God, the feeling of awe and reverence, the response of worship, and the effect of a changed moral life. Billions of people throughout the history of humanity have had some kind of religious experience of this sort.

But what about the atheist, who claims to have had no experience of God? Sometimes people want to claim that the "atheist experience of no god" counterbalances the believer's claim to have experienced God. Yet it must be noted that while the experience of something is strong evidence of that thing's existence, the absence of experience is *not* evidence of a thing's nonexistence. If you experience snow, you know that there is snow, and you can speak of what it is like. People who have not experienced snow cannot claim that there is no such thing as snow just because they have never seen it. If you have not experienced the presence of God, it only means that it is an experience yet to have.

Your Word is a lamp to my feet, and a light to my path. . . . The unfolding of Your Word gives light. It imparts understanding the simple. (Psalm 119:105,130)

All Scripture is inspired by God and is suitable for teaching, for reproof, for correction, and for training in righteousness, so that everyone who belongs to God may be proficient, equipped for every good work. (II Timothy 3:16–17)

God's Word Is a Lamp

When Karl Barth, whose dense theology was spelled out in his fourteen-volume *Church Dogmatics*,[xxxviii] finished a lecture in 1962 at the University of Chicago, he was asked by a student if he could summarize his theology in a single sentence. "Yes, I can," Barth replied. "Jesus loves me, this I know, for the Bible tells me so."[xxxix]

This indeed was the core message of Karl Barth, one of the greatest theologians of the twentieth century. We know truth about God because God reveals that truth in God's Word, the Bible.

The five traditional "proofs" of the existence of God — the ontological argument, the cosmological argument, the teleological argument, the moral argument, and the argument from religious experience — all take a philosophical path of arguing from human observation to the conclusion that God exists. The Bible mostly portrays the opposite path — it is God who reveals God's own self to humanity. People in the Biblical story do not philosophize their way to God. God comes to people, supremely in Jesus, and shows them the nature of God. The Bible is the record of this self-revelation of God.

In reality, it must be said that the five traditional proofs of God's existence are also drawing upon a self-revelation of God. The cosmological and teleological arguments are based upon nature; but nature was itself created by God; and indeed theologians have long pointed out that in addition to the book of Scripture God has given to humanity the book of Nature, which likewise reveals God's glory. The ontological argument draws upon an idea of God, which seems to have been implanted by God in the human mind. The moral argument likewise draws upon a God-implanted sense of morality, while the argument from religious experience is based upon the way that God's Spirit touches human hearts. All of these arguments are building upon some way that God has revealed God's self to humanity. But certainly the most straightforward and clear revelation of God is what is expressed in the pages of Bible, as God speaks God's truth to humanity.

But is not the Bible a human book? The Scripture itself contains the claim that it is "inspired by God." (II Timothy 3:16) But what does that mean? What sort of book is the Bible?

The extraordinary nature of the Bible is that it is not the product of a single human author writing at a particular point in time. It is the product of thousands of different people across many centuries. The earliest stories in the Bible were passed down by oral tradition — stories were handed by word of mouth from generation to generation. This was not like the "telephone game" — where something whispered around a circle morphs over time, because it is not clearly heard or remembered. Ancient oral cultures developed techniques to pass down important memories precisely. This was often done by putting a story in a fixed form, which was memorized and passed along exactly from age to age. The earliest stories in the Bible show evidence of this kind of careful oral tradition. Eventually, the stories were written down and assembled into collections, and then those collections were woven into larger works by editors. Biblical scholars believe that the Pentateuch — the first five books of the Bible — consists of four major strands of such traditions. Even as Israelite society became more literary and began to keep extensive written records — which was certainly the case by the time of the Israelite kings — there were often many people behind the production of each particular Biblical book. The books of Psalms and Proverbs, for example, contain materials from many sources, and the books of the prophets are the result not only of the words of the prophets themselves but the work of their associates to collect and edit the final book. The same pattern of broad authorship continues in the New Testament. There are four gospels; and one of the evangelists, Luke, remarks how he and others consulted many eyewitnesses. (Luke 1:1–4) The letters of the New Testament likewise come from many sources — Paul, Peter, James, John, and anonymous writers such as in the letter of Hebrews. Finally, the books of the canon — those to be considered sacred Scripture — were gradually identified over a long period of time by a large number of spiritual leaders. In the end, there are sixty-six books in the Bible, which came together across more than two millennia as the result of the work of countless storytellers, writers, collectors, and editors.

What is amazing is that the end result is one coherent story. From beginning to end, the Bible tells the story of the one God who acts according to a consistently unfolding purpose, and whose nature — though it is not always perfectly perceived by humans — is unchanging. The God of the Old Testament, who creates and who guides history, who is righteous Judge and who at the same time is gracious and merciful, and whose central characteristic is steadfast love (Hebrew: חֶסֶד *hesed*), appears in the New Testament as exactly the same God. The specific connections between different parts of the Bible are also extraordinary. Prophetic statements in the Old Testament are fulfilled centuries later in the New Testament, and key images — such as *the tree of life* or *healing waters* or *the light* or *the way* or *the Word* — appear with the same basic meanings throughout the Bible. The overall message of the Bible is likewise coherent, as people are steadily called to have faith in God, to live in love, and to find hope in God's promises. In spite of the Bible's complex origins, it is as though there is one Author over it all.

This is what is meant when it is said, late in the New Testament, that "all Scripture is inspired by God." (II Timothy 3:16) This does not mean that God directly wrote the Bible. The whole Biblical story is the story of God working through numerous human beings; so it makes sense that God would work through many human writers and editors to produce the Bible itself! But what is evident, through a careful examination of the Scriptures, is that the Spirit of God was guiding and inspiring the whole process, so that the result is a clear testimony of who God is.

The Bible is thus, as Karl Barth noted, a key way that human beings can come to know God. The Bible is the story of God revealing God's self to people through the ages, and at the same time it is a means by which the contemporary reader can hear a message from God. As the Psalmist wrote, "The unfolding of God's Word gives light; it imparts understanding to the simple." (Psalm 119:130)

But what can be said about the holy books and oral traditions of other religions? The New Testament proclaims that "Christ is the Word" (John 1) and that Christ is "the light that enlightens every person." (John 1:9) The gospel of John thus connects Christ with God's creative activity described in Genesis 1, whereby God "spoke" the universe into existence, and flooded it with light. Christ is identified as that aspect of God by which God creates, and by which God speaks; and thus it is Christ the Word who is speaking throughout the Biblical story. But the gospel also says that Christ is the light by which God "enlightens every person." This means that God has been speaking to all people in every age, enlightening them with the knowledge and truth of God. This idea that God reveals God's self universally to humanity connects directly with what has been observed in the previous "proofs" for God. God gives to people the very concept of God (ontological argument), awakens in people a sense of wonder at the glory of what God has created (teleological argument), imparts to people the principles of morality (moral argument), gives people the logical awareness to deduce that there must be an Origin to everything (cosmological argument), and arouses in people the experience of God's presence and power (the argument from religious experience). In this context, it is to be expected that the broad human awareness of God will become expressed in religion, which will provide ways for people to think about and respond to God. All religions should therefore contain something of the truth of God and provide a way for people to relate to God. At the same time, human imperfection will likely mean that the various religions will also contain distortions and limited understandings of God.

But if God is seeking to reveal God's self to humanity, it follows that this will culminate in some ultimate act of self-revelation; and this, the Scriptures declare, is precisely what happens in Jesus. The gospel of John proclaims that the Word of God, which has been speaking throughout the ages in the hearts of all people, and which has been speaking through the Biblical story, has now become incarnate in Jesus. Jesus is thus the full and perfect revelation of God's truth, the apex of the self-revelation of God through history.

With this understanding, the writings and traditions of all religions can be valued as representing something of God's truth; but the Bible is unique, as it contains the trajectory of God's self-revelation which points to and culminates in Jesus Christ. Those who read the Bible encounter the central story of how God reaches to humanity with truth and saving grace. The Bible can thus be a primary vehicle by which people come to know the reality and the power of God.

The Bible is such a powerful testimony that those who wish to deny God must also seek to discredit the Bible. But the Bible can only be disparaged by those who do not know much about it. The more one understands the Bible—the incredible nature of its origins, together with the integrity and power of its message — the more it becomes clear why this is by far the most published book in the history of humanity. The Bible speaks with extraordinary insight and depth and continual relevance, so that those who approach it with open minds will hear the word of God.

Still further, the Bible does much more than the other arguments for the existence of God. The classic proofs for God are designed to move people to acknowledge the reality of God; but the Bible is designed to bring people into connection with God — to recognize God's saving action in Jesus Christ, to respond in faith, and to experience a life-giving, hope-filled fellowship with God. When this happens, the Bible is experienced as the core, definitive "argument" for God. John Burton, in a two hundred year old hymn, put it this way:

> Holy Bible, book Divine,
> Precious treasure, thou art mine;
> Mine to tell me whence I came;
> Mine to teach me what I am.
> Mine to chide me when I rove;
> Mine to shew a Saviour's love;
> Mine art thou to guide my feet;
> Mine to judge, condemn, acquit.
> Mine to comfort in distress;
> If the Holy Spirit bless;
> Mine to shew, by living faith,
> Man can triumph over death.[xl]

Woe to you who strive with your Maker, earthen vessels with the potter! Does the clay say to the one who fashions it, "What are you making"? or "Your work has no handles"?

*Woe to anyone who says to a father, "What are you begetting?" or to a woman, "With what are you in labor?" Thus says the Lord, the Holy One of Israel, and its Maker: "Will you question me about my children, or command me concerning the work of my hands? I made the earth, and created humankind upon it; it was my hands that stretched out the heavens, and I commanded all their host...
(Isaiah 45:9–12)*

Truly, you are a God who hides himself, O God of Israel, the Savior. (Isaiah 45:15)

We are not like Moses, who put a veil over his face to keep the people of Israel from gazing at the end of the glory that was being set aside. But their minds were hardened. Indeed, to this very day, when they hear the reading of the old covenant, that same veil is still there, since only in Christ is it set aside. Indeed, to this very day whenever Moses is read, a veil lies over their minds; but when one turns to the Lord, the veil is removed. Now the Lord is the Spirit, and where the Spirit of the Lord is, there is freedom. And all of us, with unveiled faces, seeing the glory of the Lord as though reflected in a mirror, are being transformed into the same image from one degree of glory to another; for this comes from the Lord, the Spirit. (II Corinthians 3:13–18)

Why Is God Hidden

All of the proofs for God refer to some way that God is revealing God's reality to humanity. God reveals God's glory through nature, implants an awareness of God and God's goodness in the human heart, touches the human spirit with God's presence, and speaks to human beings through the Scriptures. But if God is seeking to reveal God's self to humanity, why does God not make that self-revelation more obvious? The questioning of God's existence occurs because God is still in some sense hidden from view. As the prophet Isaiah expressed it: "Truly you are a God who hides himself." (Isaiah 45:15)

Perhaps the "hiddenness" of God is in some sense due to the limitations of the human understanding. In the same passage where Isaiah speaks of the hiddenness of God, he compares humanity to a pot that cannot comprehend the purposes of the potter. God by nature is so far beyond human beings that it is to be expected that humans would have difficulty comprehending the reality of God.

Or perhaps the hiddenness of God is due even more to the hardness of the human heart. Human beings may not "see" God because they don't want to see God, but would rather pursue their own course in opposition to God. In his second letter to the Corinthians, Paul speaks of a "veil" that is between people and God, obscuring their vision of the glory of God, and he says that the veil is there because "their minds are hardened." (II Cor. 3:14) Clearly, human weakness and sinfulness play a large role in obscuring God's reality from the human mind.

Yet it seems that if God truly wished to reveal God's self to humanity, God could cut through both the limitations of the human understanding and the hardness of the human heart by simply making God's presence indisputably clear to everyone. God could appear as a giant form in the sky, or speak as a thundering voice from above, or fire down some well-placed lightning bolts whenever people did wrong; that would dispel all doubts! Such a clear self-revelation of God would also have a pronounced effect on moral turpitude, as people would likely refrain from evil deeds if it were obvious that God stood directly over them. Yet God not only refrains from such dazzling displays, but withholds any kind of undeniable communication, even from those who are seeking to communicate with God. When people pray, for example, they would love to hear a voice from God whispering in answer, but this never happens. Isaiah was right — it is not simply that God is hidden, but that "God hides himself."

But why would God withhold obvious communication when it seems that so much would be accomplished if God simply made God's presence and power indisputable? In a world in which God was undeniably at hand, people would neither question God nor disobey God. Humanity could say goodbye to both atheism and immorality.

But what sort of world would that be? What sort of freedom would people have? If God's presence were overwhelmingly obvious, people would not think to question God and would not dare to disobey God. But this means that people would essentially be puppets, cowed into submission before the Almighty. And what sort of relationship would people have with God? They would relate to God like lowly serfs before the imperial throne, giving obeisance and fealty to the overpowering Ruler whom they could not oppose and who always stood directly over them. They could hardly relate to God in faith or genuine love.

Søren Kierkegaard once wrote a parable that provides a very helpful reflection on the human situation in this regard. The parable has been retold in many forms.[xli] Imagine a powerful king who fell in love with a humble maiden in his kingdom, and who dreamed that he might marry her. He desired not simply that she would be queen, but that she might join with him in a relationship of real love. But how then should he approach her? He could, of course, ride up in his magnificent carriage, summon her from her cottage, and declare that she should become his wife. She would likely not resist; no one resisted him. But the king wished that she would love him, and love cannot be compelled. A less forceful entrance was necessary. Perhaps he should appear at her doorway, bow to her, and invite her to join him for a stroll. Of course she would be impressed. She was an ordinary maiden; she would be stunned to find the king at her door, in all his majesty! Surely she would join him. But would that be love? She might be swept along by his glory; but she would be going with him not out of love but because she was overwhelmed by his royal stature. A different approach was needed. Perhaps the king should invite her to the palace, to elevate her position — dress her in royal robes, give her a place at the royal table, and surround her with servants, so that she would feel less intimidated by the king's position. She would surely love the sumptuousness of the palace. But then how could the king know if she really loved him, or if she loved more the marvelous things he was giving her? The king appeared to be in an impossible dilemma. He desired an authentic relationship of love with the maiden; and that meant that she would need to choose to marry him out of love — a real love which was a love for him and not a reaction to his position or his wealth. But it seemed that no matter how he approached her, she would be overwhelmed by his splendor, and such love would be impossible. How could he connect with her in a genuine way?

Then the king realized the answer. He needed to conceal his royal magnificence, so that he could meet her on her level. And it had to be more than simply a temporary mask. He could not just show up in peasant garb to make her acquaintance and then whip off the costume to reveal his true magnificence. If he wanted a genuine connection, he would need to enter into her world and join in her life. So he left the palace and all his royal trappings, and moved into a simple cottage near the maiden, where he took up life as a carpenter, with the aim that she might come to know him, and, perchance, to love him.

Kierkegaard surely had in mind the words of the apostle Paul in Philippians: "Though he was in the form of God, Jesus did not regard equality with God as something to be exploited, but he emptied himself, and took the form of a servant, being born in human form." (Philippians 2:6–7)

The central thrust of the Bible is that God desires a relationship of love with human beings. But if God appeared directly in all God's glory, human beings would be intimidated and overwhelmed by God's infinite majesty. In order for people to freely choose to enter into relationship with God, God must conceal God's magnificence and come to humanity instead on a fully human level, which is exactly what God does in Jesus Christ.

This of course entails a risk. For the king, the risk was that the maiden might not choose to love him; and for God, the risk is that human beings might turn away and ignore God's overture. But such risk is necessary if human beings are to be able to respond to God freely and genuinely.

The "hiddenness" of God is exactly what must prevail in a world in which human beings are intended to be free. It is only if God is concealed from clear view that people can have the freedom to choose for or against God — to decide to join with God or not, to follow God or not, to do good or to do evil. God must "hide himself" in order for people to become independent actors in the world, whose choices — including the choice for God — will be real and meaningful. It is for the sake of human freedom and authenticity that there can be no indisputable "proofs" for God.

At the same time, if people are to be able to choose to enter a relationship with God, there must be ways in which God reveals God's care for people. The situation must be such that human beings are able to perceive the reality and love of God, while at the same time they are able to ignore and reject God. This is precisely the situation that prevails on earth; and it is this situation that is reflected in each of the classic proofs for God. Each of the arguments for God's existence points to some way in which God's reality is apparent, and yet not overwhelming. Every person is free to recognize the existence of God — through nature, or through the human concept of God, or through the human moral sense, or through religious experience, or through the witness of Scripture — or one can close one's eyes to it all. God thus reaches to humanity in a gentle fashion, so that people might respond to God not out of compulsion but freely out of love. As Paul said, "Where the Spirit of the Lord is, there is freedom." (II Cor. 3:17)

The hiddenness of God necessarily leaves room in the end for doubt and disobedience, but it is also what leaves room for an authentic response of faith and love. It is to such a response that God invites human beings; and that invitation comes to its focus in Jesus Christ, who is the perfect revelation of God's love and grace, and the full identification of God with the human condition. In the passage in II Corinthians where Paul is talking about the veil between humanity and God, he says, "In Christ the veil is set aside." (II Corinthians 3:14) When people choose to respond to God's outreach to them through Christ, then God is no longer hidden, but becomes known. As Paul says, "When one turns to the Lord, the veil is removed." (II Corinthians 3:16) Human beings on this earth, of course, can never behold the full glory of God — as Paul would say in another letter, "we see through a glass dimly" (I Cor. 13:12) — but the response of faith brings people finally into that relationship of love that God intends, in which people can know the goodness of God and live in a transforming fellowship with God. As Paul concludes, "All of us, with unveiled faces, seeing the glory of the Lord, as though reflected in a mirror, are being transformed..." (II Cor. 3:18).

After these things the word of the Lord came to Abram in a vision, "Do not be afraid, Abram, I am your shield; your reward shall be very great." But Abram said, "O Lord God, what will you give me, for I continue childless, and the heir of my house is Eliezer of Damascus?" And Abram said, "You have given me no offspring, and so a slave born in my house is to be my heir." But the word of the Lord came to him, "This man shall not be your heir; no one but your very own issue shall be your heir." He brought him outside and said, "Look toward heaven and count the stars, if you are able to count them." Then he said to him, "So shall your descendants be." And he believed the Lord; and the Lord reckoned it to him as righteousness. (Genesis 15:1–6)

Hoping against hope, Abraham believed that he would become "the father of many nations," according to what was said, "So numerous shall your descendants be." He did not weaken in faith when he considered his own body, which was already as good as dead (for he was about a hundred years old), or when he considered the barrenness of Sarah's womb. No distrust made him waver concerning the promise of God, but he grew strong in his faith as he gave glory to God, being fully convinced that God was able to do what he had promised. Therefore his faith "was reckoned to him as righteousness." (Romans 4:18–24)

The Leap of Faith

In a world in which God is necessarily hidden, in order that human beings might have genuine freedom, the proofs or arguments for God are extremely valuable; for they all point to ways in which God is gently revealing God's presence, so that people might recognize the reality of God and come into connection with God. At the same time, the very process of "proving" or arguing for the existence of God carries a risk — that people may come to think of God as a proposition to be proved, or a fact to be established. In that case, to "believe" in God would mean to agree with the proposition that God exists — to accept the idea that there is a God. In contemporary society, this is often what people mean by "believing in God."

But is God a concept to be affirmed, or a living Reality to be encountered? Throughout the history of religion, people have felt themselves drawn toward something far more than mere assent to a religious idea. People have come into a connection with God that is characterized by worship and a deep trust. This theme — that God seeks a personal fellowship with human beings — comes to its utmost expression in the Biblical story, where God reaches to people repeatedly with grace, and ultimately enters the human condition in Jesus, so that people might be brought into a direct loving relationship with God.

When Jesus therefore calls people to "believe in God" (πιστεύετε εἰς τὸν Θεόν; John 14:1), he is calling people not simply to agree with the concept that there is a God. He is inviting people into a relationship of love and trust in God. He is calling people to have faith. Some of the problem here for contemporary Americans is a language issue. If I say, "I believe you," I am saying that I accept what you are telling me as true. If I say, "I have faith in you," I am saying that I trust in you, that I have confidence in you and can rely on you. In New Testament Greek, there is one word—*pisteuo* (πιστεύω), "I believe" or "I have faith"—which means all of that. When Jesus in John 14 is talking about eternal life and says, "Believe in God" (John 14:1), or when Jesus in Matthew 17 says that "if you have faith the size of a mustard seed" you can move mountains (Matthew 17:20), or when Jesus in Mark 9 says "All things are possible for the one who believes" (Mark 9:23), or when Paul says "we are justified by faith" (Romans 5:1), or "by grace you are saved thorough faith" (Eph. 2:8), it is the same Greek word in every case that is translated "believe" or "have faith"; because the response to God for which the Scriptures call is one in which people not only acknowledge the reality of God but put their full trust in God.

A prime example of this early in the Bible can be found in the story of Abraham. God does not simply ask Abraham to affirm the idea that God exists. God calls Abraham to follow God in a journey that demands a radical trust. Abraham is to depart from his homeland and head toward an unknown country, with the promise that he will be the father of a great nation by which the whole world will one day be blessed, even though he is of advanced age and has no children at all. In response to this call, Genesis says that "Abraham believed in God." (Genesis 15:6) The Hebrew word translated "believed" is the word הֶאֱמִן (*he-e-min*, from the root verb *aman*)[xlii], which, like the Greek word *pisteuo*, means not just to accept a truth but "to rely on" or "to put one's trust in." For

Abraham, to "believe" in God meant to go with God and trust that God's promises would unfold.

When God is viewed as a concept, the human response to God is a calculation — a weighing of the evidence. If one concludes that God exists, nothing further really is required. A person can say, "I believe in God," and then go through life as though God did not matter much. In this calculus, the one who remains in charge is the human thinker, who rules on the question of the existence of God.

But when God is seen as a Person, a living Reality, then the response invited from the individual is a commitment — an entrusting of the self to God — in a relationship in which God finally is the one who holds the future. This is what is evidenced in Abraham, and later in the disciples. This is what the Bible is talking about when it speaks of believing in God, or having faith.

One of the best images for visualizing this is the image of taking a leap. Imagine that you are at the top of a high platform, looking down into a deep pool below. If you consider the situation objectively, you can conclude that if a person were to jump off that platform, the water would absorb the fall, and the person would float back up and could swim out of the pool unscathed. You can therefore believe that jumping off the platform is perfectly feasible. But it is one thing to hold such a belief; and it is quite another, while gazing into the water far below, to actually jump. To take the leap requires a trust in the sustaining power of the water, and a personal action of leaping out from the platform. It requires a kind of courage — to fling oneself into thin air.

This is what faith is. It is not simply belief in a concept of God. It is a personal movement of wholehearted commitment and reliance upon God. It is an act of entrusting one's self and one's destiny to God, so that God finally is the One in charge.

There is an inherent uncertainty in such faith. When you fling yourself off the diving platform, at that moment you are plummeting, and it is not certain just how this is going to turn out. So also with faith, at any particular moment one might not feel any sustaining force, and it may be quite unclear what the future will be. Faith involves the courage to step out, in spite of the inherent uncertainty, trusting in the power of God. This was the case with Abraham, who trusted in God, even as he seemed quite far from a good outcome. Paul said it well in his letter to the Romans:

"Hoping against hope, Abraham believed[xliii] that he would become "the father of many nations," according to what God had said . . . . He did not weaken in faith[xliv] when he considered his own body, which was already as good as dead (for he was about a hundred years old), or when he considered the barrenness of Sarah's womb. No distrust[xlv] made him waver concerning the promise of God, but he grew strong in his faith as he gave glory to God, being fully convinced that God was able to do what God had promised." (Romans 4:18–21)

Abraham's situation was very much one of inherent uncertainty, since the dream of many descendants seemed extraordinarily unlikely. There was no way to "prove" the promise; but rather, just as is the case when trusting in any person, faith was a matter of relying upon God—with a sure trust that "God is able." Abraham thus illustrated the principle well stated by D. Elton Trueblood: "Faith is not belief without proof, but trust without reservation."

Today, people often want to imagine that faith essentially means belief without sufficient evidence. Even people who believe in God will sometimes say, "You just have to take it on faith," as though faith were a matter of believing something which cannot be demonstrated. Conversely, atheists will sometimes deride believers on the grounds that believers are supposedly accepting as true something for which there is no evidence. Yet in fact there is enormous evidence for the reality of God, as noted in all of the classic arguments for God. The issue is not that people are called to believe in something

The Leap of Faith

that is unlikely. It is that they are called to trust in a Power that calls them beyond themselves.

It is significant that in the entire Biblical story, no one rejects God because there is a lack of evidence for God; but plenty of people reject God because they prefer to pursue their own agenda rather than God's. The fundamental human question is not whether God exists, but where people finally will put their trust. In the end, many people choose to put their trust in material things and earthly resources; but are such things worthy of that trust?

Nowadays the phrase "leap of faith" is often used to mean "taking a blind jump." But genuine faith is not at all blind or unreasonable. It is the standpoint of the person on the diving platform who fully considers the reality at hand. It is crucial that one sees clearly. The decisive movement is a "leap" because faith is not simply a recognition of true reality but an entrusting of the self to that reality. The critical decision is which way to leap — toward the concrete (or rocks) or toward the deep pool. In this context, the "arguments for God" are enormously important because they point people to God as the ultimate Reality — the only appropriate destination for the leap of faith.

In the presence of God and of Christ Jesus, who is to judge the living and the dead, and in view of his appearing and his kingdom, I solemnly urge you: proclaim the message; be prepared at all times to convince, rebuke, and encourage, with great patience and careful instruction. For the time is coming when people will not put up with sound doctrine, but having itching ears, they will accumulate for themselves teachers to suit their own desires, and will turn away from listening to the truth and wander away to myths. (II Timothy 4:1–4)

True Belief

Perhaps this book should have been entitled not simply "Why Believe," but "Why Believe in God," because if belief includes both what people understand to be true and where they put their trust, it is clear that everyone believes in something. Atheists believe that the universe is spiritually empty, that all things came about by pure chance, that human beings are merely animals, and that death is simply the end; and therefore they put their trust entirely in human abilities and in material resources. Everyone has beliefs. The question is whether what people believe is actually the case, and whether people are putting their trust finally in things that are truly trustworthy.

Today many people have difficulty discerning what to believe—perhaps because in this modern "information age," a great deal of purported "information" is actually bogus material, involving intentional distortions of truth. The problem is not only that there are false claims about all sorts of subjects, but that many people do not actually wish to seriously pursue the truth, and would rather simply hear what they would like to hear. In this dynamic, "reality" becomes a construct that is shaped by one's wishes, with every perception sharply refracted through the lens of existing prejudices. Instead of opinions being shaped by the facts, the facts become shaped by opinions.

This, however, is nothing new in human history. In ancient Egypt, the Pharaohs would regularly distort or rewrite history to present the "facts" as they wanted to present them. Rameses II famously ordered great epics and monuments to be created about his marvelous victory in the Battle of Kadesh — a battle which actually was a draw, and a narrow escape for Rameses from disaster. The most classic example of adjusting the facts occurred in the case of Queen Hatshepsut, who became a powerful Pharaoh of Egypt in the 15th century BC. She erected many monuments; but her successors disapproved the glory attributed to her — perhaps because they viewed her extended family as a threat, or perhaps because they simply did not like the idea of a woman Pharaoh. In any case, Pharaoh Thutmose III (her immediate successor) and then Amenhotep II declared everything about Hatshepsut to be "fake news"; and the command was given to erase her from history. This was not easy, in an age when history was chiseled in stone; but the stone workers of Egypt were put to work, and they chiseled Hatshepsut right out of every wall and monument. But they missed a few spots, which is why the world knows about Hatshepsut today. In the end, it is difficult to suppress the truth.

Nevertheless, the human pattern of wanting to distort or deny the truth, and to twist the facts to fit one's own agenda, has continued throughout time and is especially rampant today, not only in politics but in the field of religion. Internet web sites and social media channels are chock-full of false claims about religion. Those who want to deny God or create their own spin on religion seem especially inclined to promulgate false statements about the content of the Bible or about church history or about the implications of modern science for religion. Such false claims find a ready audience in a world looking for confirmation of preconceived notions. The Scripture says it well in II Timothy: "The time is coming when people will not put up with sound doctrine, but having itching ears, they will accumulate for themselves teachers to suit their own desires, and will turn away from listening to the truth and wander away into myths." (II Timothy 4:3–4) That is a pretty good description of the present day!

How then can one know what is actually true, particularly in the realm of religion? The first step is to *honestly investigate the truth*. In the second letter to Timothy, Paul encourages Timothy to "be prepared at all times to correct, rebuke and encourage, with great patience and careful instruction." (II Timothy 4:2) Earlier in the same letter, Timothy is encouraged to "study to show yourself approved unto God" (II Timothy 2:15). What is urged is careful study, with a sincere commitment to discern and communicate what is true. This kind of concern for honest and thorough investigation can be found throughout the Bible. At the beginning of the gospel of Luke, for example, Luke talks about his approach toward the life of Jesus and says, "After carefully investigating everything from the very beginning, I determined to write an orderly account, so that you may know the truth." (Luke 1:3–4) Surely what is needed to know the truth today is the same kind of careful investigation!

In doing any kind of investigation, a central principle is the importance of having *multiple reliable witnesses*. This is the case in any courtroom, and the same principle holds when considering what is true about God. In this regard, it is worth noting that each of the classic proofs for God functions as a kind of independent witness, giving clear testimony as to the reality of God. The ontological argument speaks to God's reality by pointing to the idea of God in the human mind. The cosmological argument testifies to God's existence by noting that God must be the origin of all that is. The teleological argument declares that there must be a Master Artist, namely God, behind the incredible artistry of this world. The moral argument testifies to God's reality as the source of the moral consciousness in all human beings. The argument from religious experience draws on the multiple testimonies of countless people who have had an experience of God's presence and power. The argument from Scripture points to the witness of the Bible; and the Bible itself is a compendium of many witnesses, as its sixty-six books are the product of thousands of people over time who all told the story of the one God at work through history. These major arguments for God's existence are all witnesses, each speaking from a different perspective; but in the end they all say the same thing — there is a God who reigns over all and who is at work for good.

To believe in God, therefore, is not a matter of following a whim or a personal wish. It is an act of affirming what is clearly demonstrated to be true. Still further, as noted in the previous chapter, belief involves not only an acceptance of what is true but an act of trust in what is affirmed. It is one thing, for example, to believe that the airplane can fly (based on substantial evidence); it is another to get on board. True belief in God involves not only accepting the reality of God; it is a movement of putting one's trust in God — "getting on board" with God.

Yet sometimes there is a disconnect at this point. People may accept that God is real but put their trust somewhere else — in money or social standing or personal power or influence. The Bible calls this idolatry — which is putting one's trust in something that is not God. People who are atheists are inevitably caught in idolatry, as they put their highest trust in earthly things that will inevitably fail. But the Biblical story shows that people who acknowledge God can also get lured into idolatry. The attraction of idolatry is that the idol is something near and concrete, while God may seem distant and nebulous. The downfall of idolatry is that idols cannot save.

So the Scriptures encourage people to not only accept the reality of God but to put their full trust in God. As the Psalmist says, "Put not your trust in princes [contemporary people might say "politicians"] — in mortals, in whom there is no help. Happy are those whose help is in God, whose hope is in the Lord their God — who made the heavens and the earth and the sea, and all that is in them, who keeps faith forever, who executes justice for the oppressed, who gives food to the hungry. The Lord sets people free from bondage, and opens the eyes of the blind. The Lord lifts up those who are bowed down; God shows love to the righteous." (Psalm 146:3,5-8)

It is significant that the Psalmist here encourages people to have faith in God by reminding them of who God is. Often people want to imagine that faith is a kind of substitute for knowledge — that since people cannot know whether God exists (supposedly), they therefore just have faith. But according to the Psalmist, faith is not something that comes into play because people do not know what is true. Faith, to the contrary, builds upon the knowledge of truth. It is possible in fact to have tremendous knowledge about God, because of all the ways that God reveals God's self to humanity — as noted in all the classic proofs for God — and it is precisely this knowledge about God that gives people reason to trust God. Because it is known that God is the Creator of all things, and that God is loving, and that God helps the needy and "lifts up those who are bowed down" (Psalm 146:8), human beings can confidently entrust themselves to God. In the end, faith in God is a matter of recognizing — based on all that one knows — that God alone is worthy of one's ultimate trust; and it is the rational movement of giving to God one's wholehearted devotion, to journey in life with God.

But to embark on a journey is necessarily to embark into uncertainty, because you can never know exactly how the journey will go. Here is the uncertainty of faith, that you cannot know what will come in life. But there is also a profound assurance in faith, which arises when you know you are traveling with One who is absolutely reliable. Such assurance is well exemplified in the apostle Paul as he put his full trust in Christ. He summed it up in the first part of his second letter to Timothy: "I know the One in whom I have put my trust; and I am sure that he is able to guard until the final day what I have entrusted to him." (II Timothy 1:12)

Blessed are those who do not follow the advice of the wicked, or take the path that sinners tread, or sit in the seat of scoffers; but their delight is in the law of the Lord, and on his law they meditate day and night. They are like trees planted by streams of water, which yield their fruit in its season and their leaves do not wither. In all that they do, they prosper. The wicked are not so, but are like chaff that the wind drives away.

Therefore the wicked will not stand in the judgment, nor sinners in the congregation of the righteous; for the Lord watches over the way of the righteous, but the way of the wicked will perish. (Psalm 1:1–6)

Beware of false prophets, who come to you in sheep's clothing but inwardly are ravenous wolves. You will know them by their fruits. Are grapes gathered from thorns, or figs from thistles? In the same way, every good tree bears good fruit, but the bad tree bears bad fruit. (Matthew 7:15–17)

Belief Matters

In seventeenth-century France, Blaise Pascal developed one of the more unique and memorable arguments for why a person should believe. In France at the time, gambling was very popular, and Pascal himself was quite involved in the gaming world. He once helped a prominent gambler figure out why he was losing at a dice game (in the process helping to develop modern probability theory), and he invented the roulette wheel. So when it came to putting forth an argument for why people should believe in God, Pascal played off of the popularity of gambling and put forth an argument that was essentially this:

Consider the biggest bet of all time. It is the wager as to whether God exists. Suppose you are quite uncertain as to which way it will go—maybe God exists, or maybe not. It is like flipping a coin, and you do not know which side will come up. But in the case of God's existence, you must place a bet. You either believe in God, or you do not. You have to choose; and in this case, you are betting your life. Now consider what the outcome of this wager might be. If you bet that there is a God and you are right, you gain eternity, because you have staked your life on God. If you are wrong, you gain nothing and die; but if there is no God, you were going to lose your life anyways. On the other hand, if you bet that there is not a God and you are right, you still gain nothing; you die. If you are wrong, you inherit death when you could have inherited eternal life! So in this wager, you have everything to gain in betting on God, and nothing finally to lose. The rational person, said Pascal, will bet everything on God.

This whole argument is now known as Pascal's wager. It is a line of argumentation entirely different from that of the classic proofs for God, which all consider what a human being can reasonably know about God, and what a person can infer from all the evidence at hand. Pascal's argument is based not on the grounds for belief but on the results of belief. The reason to believe, he argued, is because your belief will have eternal consequences.

Most people who believe in God, especially those who have seriously considered the proofs for God, will insist that belief in God has a foundation far more solid and sure than the outcome of flipping a coin! But Pascal's wager can serve to turn attention to a very important reality—belief matters. It matters enormously for one's destiny.

In the Bible, one of the most succinct declarations of the consequences of belief in God can be found in Psalm 1, which declares, "Blessed is the one— אַשְׁרֵי הָאִישׁ —whose delight is in the ways of the Lord. That person is like a tree planted by streams of water, which yields its fruit in season, and its leaves do not wither. The wicked are not so, but are like chaff that the wind drives away. The wicked will not stand in the judgment, nor sinners in the congregation of the righteous; for the Lord watches over the way of the righteous, but the way of the wicked will perish." (Psalm 1)

This short Psalm details four central consequences of faith for the believer. The believer, first of all is "blessed"—the first word in the Psalm. This word in Hebrew (*ashar*) can also be translated "happy," but it means much more than a fleeting feeling. It indicates a state of wholeness, well-being, and spiritual health—those qualities that make for true and lasting happiness in life.

The second consequence is that the believer is "like a tree planted by the water... whose leaves do not wither." In the semi-arid lands of the ancient near east, where a tree could easily wither in a drought, this image of the tree planted by water suggests that the believer has a never-ending source of strength and sustenance in the face of trying times. The believer is not necessarily spared adversity, but can find — through believing — the power to persevere through it.

The third consequence is that the believer "bears fruit" — a Biblical image for doing good. Believers are inspired and empowered to bring real blessing to the world.

Finally, believers have an ultimate destiny that is the opposite of the destiny of the wicked, who "will perish." The implication of the Psalm, which is brought to great clarity and emphasis in Jesus, is that those who have faith in God will inherit an eternal reward. As Jesus said, "Everyone who hears my word and believes in God who sent me has eternal life." (John 5:24)

These four consequences — spiritual wholeness, strength through adversity, the ability to make a positive impact with one's life, and the promise of life eternal — are enormous; and they repeatedly appear throughout the Bible as the real consequences of faith. In response, therefore, to the question, "Why Believe?" a major answer is: "Because it makes a tremendous positive difference in one's personal life!" This is sometimes called the pragmatic answer to the question. One believes because of the actual effect that belief has on life.

This effect can be seen in many aspects of life. What difference does it make, for example, if you believe that all people are of infinite worth in God's eyes? There have been societies in history which have not believed that, and which have treated people accordingly. But if you do believe that all people are of infinite value to God, then you will treat all people with respect and care. What you believe matters for how you live your life.

The effect of belief can be noted not only in the realm of personal life but also on a broad social scale. Historically, belief in God has had a huge positive impact on societies at large. Look at colleges, for example, around the world, and you will find that a great many of them were founded by people who were motivated by their faith. The same is true of numerous hospitals. Look at the homeless shelters, clothing centers, food banks, and free clinics in towns across America. In most cases — in fact, in nearly all cases — they were started by and continue to be staffed and funded by people of faith. Look at the twelve-step groups in any community. They were founded in faith — grounded in the importance of relying on a "higher power" to overcome addiction — and their most typical meeting space is in churches. Look at charitable giving overall, supporting a vast range of critically important undertakings; it is people of faith who are giving by far the lion's share.

Or look beyond such tangible measures at the effect of religious belief on the overall values of a society. In America up to this day, the most important values that permeate the culture have their rooting in the Bible — and in the people of faith who throughout American history were promoting those values as an expression of their faith. Here are a few Biblical values that have made their way into American culture:

1) The society should ensure that the poor do not go hungry (see, for example, the gleaning laws of the Old Testament)
2) People should be provided with shelter who have none (note Old Testament laws about hospitality, or not taking someone's cloak overnight)
3) Special help should be given to the elderly and to orphans (this is a huge point of emphasis among the prophets, who, when thinking of the elderly, were thinking especially about widows, who had no means of self-support)

4) All people should be viewed equally as children of God (see the creation story in Genesis, and later New Testament comments that "we are all one in Christ")
5) If people are judged guilty of wrongdoing, they should not simply be irretrievably condemned but should be given opportunity to redeem themselves (this principle receives particular emphasis in Jesus, but there are also elements of this principle in some Old Testament laws)
6) Foreigners should be treated with compassion (this is accented at several points in the Old Testament, such as Exodus 22:21, which says, "Do not mistreat or oppress a foreigner, for you were foreigners in Egypt")
7) Societies should strive to live in peace (this is another major point of emphasis in the prophets)
8) Rulers are not above the law but are subject to it (this was clear for all Israelite kings)
9) Workers should be given regular time off to rest (this is embedded in the Sabbath law)
10) There should be respect for each person's property (this is well grounded in multiple Old Testament laws)
11) People should treat one another with mercy (this principle runs strongly from the Old Testament to the New)
12) Everyone should make some personal sacrifices in order to bring help and benefit to others (the tithing rule incorporated this principle in Old Testament times, and Jesus vastly expanded the principle in the New Testament)

Many people in America today would affirm these values without realizing that they all come straight out of the Bible. Of course, people of other religions have discerned a number of the same values, drawing on their own God-given moral consciousness. The point is that these values prevail in American culture because people of faith in years past were motivated to strongly advance such values and to inculcate these principles in the society at large. Such values do not necessarily prevail in a culture. American society has the particular moral character that it has because of the impact of religious belief.

What happens, then, if belief fades? Many people nowadays want to say that belief in God is not needed in order for a society to have strong and positive values. They can point to the fact that even as church participation has faded in recent decades, many people continue to live by good values, such as the importance of helping the needy or treating other people with compassion, or the value of seeking peace for the world and harmony among all peoples. They do not seem to realize that those values have come out of religious belief and have been carried to the present because of the witness of believers; and when people today absorb the values without the belief, they are simply riding on the moral momentum of the religious belief of ages past. Belief in God has been the engine that has driven the moral development of American society. If the engine is removed, the momentum of the past will carry things forward for awhile. But what happens when the momentum fades? There is no particular reason for those moral values over the long term to hold.

Belief matters. It matters what people believe, and it matters when they help others to come to faith, because that belief will make an enormous difference in their personal lives and in the society at large. At the same time, it must be noted that belief will have a positive impact only when it is *true belief*—belief that involves an affirmation of what is actually true, and a genuine trust in God. False belief, conversely, can bring very negative consequences. In the past century, the false ideologies of fascism and communism wreaked havoc on the earth; and today a very twisted view of Islam, embodied by al Qaeda and ISIS, likewise demonstrates that false belief can result in tremendous evil. This of course reaffirms the central principle—*what people believe matters*.

Jesus encapsulated this principle in the Sermon on the Mount, in his classic illustration about good or bad trees and how they bring corresponding fruits. As he said, "Are grapes gathered from thorns, or figs from thistles? In the same way, every good tree bears good fruit, but the bad tree bears bad fruit." (Matthew 7:16–17) It is significant in verse 17 that in the original Greek, two different words are used for "good" and two different words for "bad." In the phrase, "good" tree, the Greek word used is ἀγαθός (*agathos*), which indicates something that is intrinsically good, or good in its essential character. In "good" fruit, the Greek word used is καλὸς (*kalos*), which indicates something outwardly beautiful or good in appearance. Likewise in the phrase, "bad" tree, the Greek word used is σαπρός (*sapros*), which basically means rotten, while in "bad" fruit the Greek word is πονηρός (*poneros*), which indicates something that is wicked or that brings pain and trouble. The basic idea in each case is that the fundamental inner character of something inevitably produces a corresponding outward result.

A person's belief—what one holds to be true and right and where one puts trust—constitutes a person's fundamental inner orientation, and this will inevitably bear fruit of one kind or another. This does not mean that all "bad fruit" is the same or that all good fruit is the same. Jesus' words about grapes and thorns and figs and thistles call to mind the fact that in any garden there are all sorts of plants. Some might be troublesome, like thorns and thistles; some might be dangerous, like poison ivy or plants with poisonous fruit; and some be just be useless, producing nothing of value. Similarly, there are all sorts of false belief systems—from political extremism to religious fanaticism to atheism—which produce "bad fruit" of all different kinds. Some beliefs bring very toxic and dangerous results, and others simply produce little of value. But from the gardening perspective, it is all "bad fruit" in that it does not contribute anything good to the garden.

In Matthew 7, Jesus' words about the good and bad fruit are part of a basic warning against false teaching. You can recognize false teaching, Jesus says, by looking at its fruit—something quite evident today when one looks at a movement such as ISIS. Jesus' central point to his listeners is that they need to hold to true belief; for it is only when one has authentic faith in God that one becomes like that tree in Psalm one—which flourishes even through tough times and which truly and lastingly bears good fruit.

But if true belief is so critical, both for one's own destiny and that of the larger community, how does one know exactly what true belief is? This will be the subject of the last chapter.

Then Paul stood in front of the Areopagus and said, "Athenians, I see how extremely religious you are in every way. For as I went through the city and looked carefully at the objects of your worship, I found among them an altar with the inscription, 'To an unknown god.' What therefore you worship as unknown, this I proclaim to you. The God who made the world and everything in it, he who is Lord of heaven and earth, does not live in shrines made by human hands, nor is he served by human hands, as though he needed anything, since he himself gives to all mortals life and breath and all things. From one ancestor God made all nations to inhabit the whole earth, and he allotted the times of their existence and the boundaries of the places where they would live, so that they would search for God and perhaps grope for him and find him—though indeed he is not far from each one of us. For 'In him we live and move and have our being'; as even some of your own poets have said, 'For we too are his offspring.' Since we are God's offspring, we ought not to think that the deity is like gold, or silver, or stone, an image formed by the art and imagination of mortals. While God has overlooked the times of human ignorance, now he commands all people everywhere to repent, because he has fixed a day on which he will have the world judged in righteousness by a man whom he has appointed, and of this he has given assurance to all by raising him from the dead. (Acts 17:22–31)

The Way, the Truth, and the Life

It has become quite apparent in the present day that it is not enough to believe in "God." It is important to have a clear understanding of who God truly is! When terrorists shout "God is great" while gunning down innocent people, most people would say that they have an utterly false notion of God. But how then does one come assuredly to a true picture of God?

The apostle Paul addressed this question in a very enlightening way in his speech to the people of Athens, recorded in the book of Acts. The Athenians at the time were the philosophical heirs of Plato and Aristotle, and most of them strongly affirmed a divine reality. As Paul noted at the outset of his speech to them, "I perceive that you are very religious." (Acts 17:22) The Greek notion of divinity held that there are multiple gods; and Paul observed in the city that the Greeks were so intent on honoring all the gods that they had even erected an altar inscribed, "To an unknown god" (Acts 17:23) — just in case they missed one.

Paul affirmed the authenticity of their spiritual quest and their general awareness of God. He approvingly quoted Greek poets, who had said "In God we live and move and have our being" (Acts 17:28)[xlvi] and "We are indeed God's offspring." (Acts 17:28).[xlvii] He referred to the well-known cosmological argument, which had its origins in both Plato and Aristotle, as he talked about "the God who made the world and everything in it" (Acts 17:24), and he acknowledged the validity of widespread religious experience, as he talked about how people "seek God, in the hope that they might feel after God and find God" (Acts 17:27). Paul thus affirmed the basic premise that is reflected in all of the classic proofs for God—human beings everywhere have the ability to come to know the reality of God, and can enter thereby into a real connection with God.

At the same time, Paul asserted that the specific understanding that the Greeks had of God was still incomplete and flawed. He referred to the Greek practice of having numerous statues of gods and said, "We ought not to think that the Deity is like gold or silver or stone, a representation by human art and imagination." (Acts 17:29) The basic perspective shown forth by Paul is that various religions are not to be condemned, but rather are to be honored for their awareness of God; while at the same time it must be acknowledged that in diverse ways they often come to misconceptions about the nature of God.

How, then, can human beings arrive at a true picture of God? Paul's central point, reflected at many places in the New Testament, is that God reveals the perfect picture of God's reality in Jesus Christ. But how can one know that Jesus is the perfect self-revelation of God? There are many elements that testify to Jesus' identity. The extraordinary miracles of Jesus, the sublime nature of his teaching, the moral perfection of his character, the way that he fulfilled ancient scriptures, and the spiritual authority he embodied all point to his identity as the Messiah—the one who reveals God fully to humanity. But Paul finally stated that there is one element that absolutely establishes Jesus as the culmination of God's self-revelation. As Paul said at the conclusion of his speech to the Athenians, "God has fixed a day on which God will judge the world in righteousness by a man whom He has appointed [namely, Jesus], and of this God has given assurance to all people by raising Jesus from the dead." (Acts 17:31)

The resurrection is the absolute confirmation that God has acted through Jesus to bring humanity to a complete and right relationship with God. But how can one know that the resurrection is not simply a pious legend? There is tremendous evidence for the reality of the resurrection. It has been historically established that reports of the resurrection arose very quickly after the crucifixion of Jesus. Legends typically take much longer to emerge. At the heart of those reports was the fact that the tomb in which Jesus had been buried was found empty. It is significant that none of the early opponents of Christianity ever disputed the fact that the tomb was empty. They never doubted that Jesus had in fact died during the crucifixion — no one survived Roman crucifixion — and they admitted that the tomb was empty; but they suggested that the body of Jesus must have been stolen. Yet the reports of the resurrection also include many reports of resurrection appearances of the Risen Jesus, and these reports came from hundreds of eyewitnesses. Moreover, those who want to suggest that the resurrection must have been a hoax have to reckon with the fact that those early witnesses of the resurrection went on to devote the rest of their lives to spreading the message about the Risen Jesus, often at great sacrifice. Would people devote their lives to something they knew was a hoax? The tremendous commitment of the early apostles shows that they were absolutely sure that Jesus, who was dead, is now alive.

The reports of the resurrection in the gospels also have a number of quite notable features, which all point to their authenticity. All four gospels report that women were the first eyewitnesses of the empty tomb. In the first century Jewish world, which was heavily patriarchal, women were not considered to be the most reliable witnesses.[xlviii] Anyone concocting a story at the time would never say that the primary witnesses were women! The fact that the gospels do report that all the initial eyewitnesses were women indicates that the gospel writers were not inventing their material but were reporting the actual events. The women are also named, indicating that they were known in the community at the time when the gospels were written. This points to another important feature of the gospels — they were written within the decades when many eyewitnesses were still living, who would have been both a source of accurate and credible memories and a check against any false reporting. Still another key feature of the resurrection accounts in the gospels is that while all four gospels agree as to the central elements — the empty tomb, the stone rolled away, the women witnesses, the appearance of Jesus, and so forth — they also differ in many of the particular details recounted. This corresponds with the nature of authentic testimony. When different witnesses give reports about some surprising event, they will generally recall different details and will describe the event somewhat differently, but will agree on the key features of the event. The four gospel accounts of the resurrection have precisely this characteristic of authentic testimonies — each tells the story a bit differently, but they all agree on the central elements. If different witnesses were to give precisely the same description of an event, one would suspect that they colluded with one another! The variations in the gospel accounts, along with their central agreements, thus point to the veracity of the gospels as genuine testimonies to the resurrection of Jesus.

The final proof for God is the resurrection — for it is a demonstration of the power of God and the truth of everything that Jesus proclaimed about God. Furthermore, the resurrection confirms that God has acted most centrally in Jesus. This means that while people may come to acknowledge the reality of God through many avenues, there is one place where people can see the perfect picture of who God is, there is one person in whom people can find the ideal model for how they should live, and there is one point where God has acted decisively to bring eternal salvation to all humanity—in Jesus Christ. As Jesus said, "I am the way, the truth, and the life." (John 14:6)

Paul thus called the Athenians to move beyond their basic belief in God to believe in Jesus as God's Messiah and the Savior of humankind. The Scriptures call every person to do the same. As the gospel of John—at the conclusion of its resurrection accounts—declares, "These are written so that you may believe that Jesus is the Christ, the Son of God, and that believing you may have life in his name." (John 20:31)

Epilogue

The most brilliant minds in human history have recognized the reality of God. Belief is not contrary to reason. A reasonable consideration of all aspects of the universe leads directly to the conclusion that there is a "higher power" — namely God — behind all that is. As Albert Einstein declared, "Everyone who is seriously involved in the pursuit of science becomes convinced that a spirit is manifest in the laws of the universe—a spirit vastly superior to that of man, and one in the face of which we with our modest powers must feel humble."[xlix]

If people doubt or deny God, it is often because they cannot "see" God in the world. Faith is indeed, as the Scriptures say, "the conviction of things not seen." (Hebrews 11:1) Yet the most fundamental aspects of reality are things not seen! Einstein's central theories described elements of the universe that people not only could not see but often had a hard time imagining. Quantum physics makes plain that what you see when you look at a solid object is not actually what is there; the subatomic reality is something other than what meets the eye. Belief in God involves moving past the material surface of things and embracing what is ultimately Real.

This movement or "leap" of faith is by no means blind. Just as scientists establish the true nature of the unseen physical universe by a careful examination of the evidence, so one can discern the spiritual nature of the universe by means of a thorough examination of the evidence. This is what is done through all of the "proofs" or arguments for God. In the end, the evidence for God is overwhelming.

Yet the process of discerning the reality of God is also different from the process of investigating the material universe, in that the physical universe is just passively there to be discovered, while God is a living Reality who is actively seeking a relationship with human beings. While God is necessarily cloaked with a kind of "hiddenness," in order to preserve human freedom, God reveals God's presence and nature to human beings in numerous ways, as noted in the previous chapters. The human awareness of God is actually a response to God's self-revelation — an "opening of the eyes" to perceive the reality of God.

In this context, it is to be expected that God's self-revelation will coalesce in some point where God perfectly reveals God's nature and God's will and design for humanity. That point is Jesus Christ. As Jesus said, "If you know me, you know my Father also; from now on you have known Him and seen Him." (John 14:7)

When people say that they do not believe in God, often what they do not believe in is a distorted picture of God that they were given at some point in their past. They do not believe in a God who is an old man in the sky, or a God who brings torments upon people or who despises certain people, or a God who devises endless rules for people. Such distorted images of "god" deserve unbelief! True belief takes shape when people look to Jesus Christ and take hold of the reality of God that is conveyed through Christ; for it is in Christ that one sees fully the love and grace that God is pouring out to all humanity.

God is not dead.[1] From Nietzsche's proclamation that "God is dead"[li] in the late nineteenth century to the "death of God" movement in the 1960's, people have announced the vanishing of God from the modern world. But God does not disappear, despite what people may at times imagine; and God continues to reach to a wayward humanity, so that people might find genuine life and eternal blessing as they put their faith in God. So the Scriptures proclaim, "May the God of hope fill you with all joy and peace in believing..."[lii]

Notes

Chapter 1
i. A good example of this is Tim Whitmarsh, *Battling the Gods: Atheism in the Ancient World*, 2016.

Chapter 2
ii. Anselm, *Proslogion*.
iii. René Descartes, *Meditation* V.
iv. Immanuel Kant, *Critique of Pure Reason*. Also Bertrand Russell, *Introduction to Mathematical Philosophy*, 1919.
v. David Hume, *The Natural History of Religion*, 1757.
vi. Ludwig Feuerbach, *Das Wesen des Christentums* (*The Essence of Christianity*), 1841. *Das Wesen der Religion* (*The Essence of Religion*), 1846. *Erläuterungen und Ergänzungen zum Wesen des Christentums*, 1846, *Theogonie*, 1847.
vii. Sigmund Freud, *Totem and Taboo*, 1913. *The Future of an Illusion*, 1927.
viii. Paul Tillich, *Systematic Theology*, 1951–63.

Chapter 3
ix. Aristotle, *Metaphysics*, Beta, 4.
x. Thomas Aquinas, *Summa Theologica*, Third Article.
xi. Ibid.
xii. See, for example, Gottfried Wilhelm Leibniz, *Monadology*.
xiii. David Albert, "New York Times Book Review" (March 25, 2012) Albert notes numerous other fundamental flaws in the book.
xiv. Fred Hoyle, "The Universe: Past and Present Reflections." *Engineering and Science*, (November, 1981) pp. 8–12.

xv. Owen Gingerich, "Dare a Scientist Believe in Design," in *Evidence of Purpose* (New York: Continuum Publishing, 1994), p. 23. The same observation is made by Stephen Hawking.

xvi. Stephen Hawking, *A Brief History of Time* (New York: Bantam Books, 1988), p. 125.

xvii. Paul Davies, "The Unreasonable Effectiveness of Science," in *Evidence of Purpose*, p. 49.

xviii. Gingerich, op. cit.

xix. Thomas Hertog, Interview with the European Research Council, May 2, 2018.

xx. S.W. Hawking and Thomas Hertog, "Journal of High Energy Physics" (April, 2018).

xxi. Stephen Hawking, *The Grand Design* (New York, Bantam Books, 2010).

Chapter 4

xxii. "Saturday Evening Post" (Oct. 26, 1929), p.17.

xxiii. William Paley, *Natural Religion*, 1802.

xxiv. Fred Hoyle, *The Intelligent Universe* (New York: Holt, Rinehart and Winston, 1984).

xxv. Ibid.

xxvi. Bonaventure, *The Soul's Journey into God*, trans. by Ewert Cousins (Paulist Press: 1978), pp. 15, 67–68.

Chapter 5

xxvii. *Mahābhārata* Shānti-Parva 167:9.

xxviii. Shayast-na-Shayast 13:29

xxix. *Udanavarga* 5:18

xxx. Confucius, *Analects*, XV, 24.

xxxi. Isocrates, *Nicocles or the Cyprians*.

xxxii. Immanuel Kant, *Critique of Pure Reason*.

xxxiii. Hastings Rashdall, *The Theory of Good and Evil*, 1907.

xxxiv. C. S. Lewis, *Mere Christianity*, 1952.

Chapter 6
xxxv.   Friedrich Schleiermacher, *Der christliche Glaube nach den Grundsätzen der evangelischen Kirche*, 1821–1822.
xxxvi.   William James, *Varieties of Religious Experience: a Study in Human Nature*, 1902.
xxxvii.   Many centuries after Jacob, a legend emerged that this stone somehow made its way to Scotland where it became the Stone of Scone, used for the coronation of Scottish and then British monarchs. It is a quaint legend, with absolutely no historical foundation.

Chapter 7
xxxviii.   Karl Barth, *Kirchliche Dogmatik*,1932–1967. Specifically, this massive series has four "volumes," with a total of twelve "parts," one of which is split into two halves, plus an index.
xxxix.   Barth had learned the German version as a youth — "Jesus liebt mich, ganz gewiß, denn die Bibel sagt mir dies. Alle Kinder schwach und klein, lädt er herzlich zu sich ein."
xl.   John Burton, Sr., *Youth's Monitor in Verse*, 1803.

Chapter 8
xli.   Kierkegaard's actual parable, written in the dense and rather convoluted style that is characteristic of Kierkegaard, is found in his *Philosophical Fragments*, pp. 31–43. What is offered here is a retelling of the basic idea.

Chapter 9
xlii.   This is the hiphil form of the root verb אָמַן — *aman*
xliii.   Again the word is ἐπίστευσεν, the past tense (aorist) of the Greek verb, *pisteuo*.
xliv.   τῇ πίστει — in faith. The Greek word here for faith is *pistis*, the noun form of the verb *pisteuo*.
xlv.   ἀπιστίᾳ — *apistia*. The word translated "distrust" is a negative of the word *pistis*.

Chapter 12

xlvi. Epimenides, *Cretica*.

xlvii. Aratus, *Phaenomena*.

xlviii. Cf. Josephus, *Antiquities of the Jews*, 4.219, where Josephus enumerates a basic rule as follows: "Let not the testimony of women be admitted."

Epilogue

xlix. Albert Einstein, from a 1936 response to a child who asked in a letter if scientists pray. Quoted in *Albert Einstein, The Human Side* (Princeton: Princeton University Press, 2013), pp. 32–33.

l. The phrase, "God is dead" ("Gott ist tot") was proclaimed by Friedrich Nietzsche in his book, *Die fröhliche Wissenschaft* (1882). The phrase denoted for Nietzsche the loss of belief in God in western civilization.

li. Nietzsche's "God is dead" idea was especially popularized through his major work, *Also sprach Zarathustra* (1883–85).

lii. Romans 15:13a

www.ingramcontent.com/pod-product-compliance
Lightning Source LLC
Chambersburg PA
CBHW020945090426
42736CB00010B/1278